HOLIDAY INN MOTEL was founded in Memphis, Tennessee by three men. It was my privilege to know each one of these men personally.

One of the men, the author of this book, Bill Walton, was in my class all through grade school, Junior high and high school.

He was President of Holiday Inns for many years, but because, of his convictions concerning installing "HBO" movies in Hoiday Inns-and because he voted "NO" concerning Holiday Inn entering the Casino business in Atlantic City,he was relieved of the responsibility of "President" and finally removed from all responsibilities. However, God has turned defeat into victory for him.

May the Lord bless this reading in your life.

                    Geneva Long Dawkins
                          and
                    Terrell Dawkins

Inn Keeper

Inn Keeper

WILLIAM B. WALTON
with MEL LORENTZEN
authors of *The New Bottom Line*

 Tyndale House
Publishers, Inc.,
Wheaton, Illinois

First printing, October 1987

Library of Congress
Catalog Card Number 87-50625
ISBN 0-8423-1615-9
Printed in the United States of America

For my children,
William, Kackie, Rusty, and Geneen,
who survived their father's career
and turned out all right,
thanks to the grace of God

CONTENTS

INTRODUCTION
Where I'm Coming From,
and Where I'm Taking You

If your life seems to be uphill all the way, count yourself among the blessed! You may feel exhausted sometimes by the daily routine. You may wonder if you'll ever make any headway against the obstacles in your path. You may even question now and then whether God really had any clear purpose in mind when he put you here.

Take it from me, you do matter. God wouldn't have set you on such a steep trail to heaven without your best interests in mind, but that's not so you can show off your climbing ability.

Instead, it's to prove to this unbelieving world what he can do with ordinary people like you and me when we let him display his extraordinary power to get us from the lowlands of human limitations to the highlands of heaven's splendors.

As the President of the largest corporation in the history of its industry, I have been in a position to witness the rise and fall of many promising careers, both in "my" own company and in others. Sometimes I've seen gifted young people with stars in their eyes make utter fools of themselves and fail hopelessly.

Other times I've seen scared and doubting men and women take on the impossible and give it a knockout punch they never thought they could deliver.

What is the one factor that makes all the difference? It's not talent or training. It's not having the right connections or getting the breaks. It's not even hard work, by itself, although without it chances for success are dim. What really separates "top people" from "flop people" is *outlook*. Whenever and wherever you spot an achiever, you find a person whose point of view is right. From housewife to movie star, from university student to business tycoon, it's ultimately their *attitude* that will settle their destiny.

Those people have not been spared the tough tests that come to all of us. They haven't been "lucky," as some would put it, in escaping trouble and hardship. Again I say, the fact that I was overseeing the daily operations of a multinational corporation, which was recognized by everybody to be nothing less than a modern business miracle, had its full quota of thorns for me, scratching and stabbing me relentlessly even while I reaped a few roses along the way. It was a steep and rocky path I was climbing, which got harder to maneuver the higher I went. A lot more than I ever let on to anyone, I agonized with the ache and gasped with the effort to keep going. I'm not trying to sound heroic. I just want to caution some unsuspecting dreamer that climbing takes a lot more out of you than you might expect.

If you've been over that course in any of life's callings, whatever your acknowledged—and even honored— accomplishments might be, you have unavoidably experienced the inward personal trauma of insecurity. Sometimes you have been at the point of panic, when your position is threatened by outside forces, or your self-control gets shaky. You have felt your knees buckle with disappointments. You have bloodied your knuckles fighting for what you believed in. You have even known the painful spasms of heart when a trusted associate turns traitor or a loved one walks out on you.

For twenty years I was chief operating officer of an enterprise that began with four "experimental" motels in Memphis, Tennessee, which spawned the worldwide network of Holiday Inns, Inc. The enterprise eventually numbered nearly 2,000 company and franchise establishments in fifty countries, approached gross annual revenues of $2 billion, hosted some 250,000 guests every night of the year, supplied jobs for about 150,000 people, and became a household word synonymous with hospitality to traveling families and business people. It was a fabulous adventure worth every bit of the inevitable frustration we all bump into, whatever our occupation.

But I also wear the scars of an exploded dream. People in the business world today are so obsessed with survival in the system that they are unaware, as I was for a long time, of many clear symptoms of impending disaster. They do not know that the mentality and motivation to drive for success at all costs are self-defeating and even self-destructive. The cliches of "reaching the top" or "making it big" are so common-place that pitfalls and booby traps lining the route are ignored or overlooked. And that potential for disaster lurks everywhere, from parenting to preaching, for the simple reason that no one is exempt from the temp-tation to get priorities out of order.

There is a particular reason, though, why I want to install an "early warning system" about dangers ahead. It's embarrassing as well as sad to say that Christians, who have to earn their living in this world, perform daily duties that can get downright dull a lot of times. Even though they know God is preparing them by his Spirit for a glorious Kingdom in the world to come, too often they seem to be victimized by the negative forces as readily as anybody else.

I'm not talking just about men and women of faith who have jobs out in the general marketplace, where they surely are exposed constantly to peer pressure and to professional practices that run contrary to God's purposes. I include everybody—young and old, in home

or school or job or even church—who is vulnerable to
the deceptions about success. Catastrophe can come,
even within the cause of Christ, to anyone of us who
lets down his guard for a moment, or compromises on
seemingly little points, or simply forgets that God's way
and the world's way are opposites.

You can come to a clear understanding of that, of
course, by careful study of the Scriptures. Much of the
time, though, what we hear from the pulpit in our local
churches, or share in our neighborhood Bible study
groups, strikes us as abstract, as rather remote from
what we have to face in the daily grind. Most of us are
readily willing to witness to our faith in Christ as
Savior and Lord. Some of us even dare to rise up and do
battle for the authority of the Bible as the Word of God.
But if someone really forced us to analyze how
practical it all is with reference to on-the-job realities
wherever we work, a lot of us would be pretty hard-
pressed to make a good case for putting spiritual
principle first in every situation.

Actually, sometimes without knowing it, or sometimes
without admitting it, we have adjusted our religious
belief system to the world's operational system so that
the conflict is at least minimized if not eliminated.

Think about what we have in that authoritative
spiritual Operations Manual of ours, the Bible. It is a
storybook, in the finest sense of that term, uniquely
inspired by the Holy Spirit of God, but nevertheless
filled with accounts of real flesh-and-blood people who
faced real down-to-earth situations and had to do real
hand-to-hand combat with the forces of evil that are
loose in the world and largely run things. It depicts
with raw honesty the miserable consequences we
brought on ourselves, both as the human race and as
responsible individuals, by our disobedience to the good
will of God, which he plainly communicated in the
beginning to insure our enjoyment of all his beautiful
creation as well as the pleasure of his companionship.

Now, I don't pretend to rank up there with the saints
and heros of Scripture, whose exploits nerve us for the

battles we have to face by showing us the faithfulness and sufficiency of God in their lives. But I am a modern businessman who is a Christian at work in the everyday world. I, too, have had to learn the hard way that the path of righteousness we are commanded to follow is plagued with all kinds of snares. I, too, have had to face things about myself as a person, and about my conduct of affairs in the places where the Lord has assigned me, that are not easy to confront, much less to tell to others.

You see, I set my sights on climbing the success mountain when I was a very young boy, because of circumstances that arose in our family. And for the next half century I held to an undeviating course upward that I fully expected would bring me to the top of my profession. I could picture myself straddling the peak of my Mount Everest of business achievement, proudly planting there the victor's pennant inscribed with a bold "W.B.W." that would make my ancestors, as well as my family and friends, proud that I had made it in such grand style.

But, did I make it to the top of my mountain? Are you going to make it to the top of yours?

If you're willing to read my story, I'll promise you this much: You will learn some secrets about survival that may make all the difference between a climb to conquest that will matter to you forever, or a climb that wastes the best God has made you capable of becoming, regardless of intoxicating applause from your worldly admirers.

I firmly believe God designed and equipped us for an exhilarating climb, not for a slump-shouldered shuffle that barely gets us through the wilderness of existence from one stagnant waterhole to another. What is the purpose of his Word speaking of our mounting up with wings like eagles to the craggy pinnacles piercing the clouds if he actually meant instead for us to stay underground and tunnel mole-like through dirt and darkness?

One warning, though: The devil, whom the Bible

characterizes as a liar and a deceiver, can pervert
mountaintop experiences to destroy us, just as he tried
to do with Jesus himself. Bill Walton's mountain turned
out to be a crest of crisis that threatened everything I
believed in.

So, let me tell you the whole truth about my climb,
which happened to be in the business world. I pray that
God will use this story to challenge you to watch your
every step while you stretch for heights in your
vocation that you might never have imagined could be
within your reach.

1 ★ Crash!

When I was twelve, "Boss" Ed Crump, the Memphis political power broker, said to me, "Son, I'll make you into a senator. You're a natural!"

I needed that. It was 1932, and my depression-beaten father had driven off alone one day in the family car, never to return home. When we had moved to Memphis around 1921 from my birthplace in Pine Bluff, Arkansas, his prospects were first-rate. He was in banking and started his own mortgage company in the mid-twenties. In those better years, my mother, Katherine, reveled in her glittering socialite role as the pretty wife of a promising young investment banker. The two of them were on the go a lot, always a popular couple at business functions and parties. Even their little boy Billy got his picture on the society pages a few times for winning baby contests!

We were a two-car family back then, the big blue Buick my mother drove, and my dad's Ford Model A—the first to roll off the Memphis plant's assembly line. I still remember how snooty I felt when we rode around town and everybody pointed at that spanking new Walton car.

Our house on Linden Avenue was a nice one, in a pleasant section of the city just around the corner from venerable St. Luke's Episcopal Church. There Miss Brame presided over kindergarten school and bolstered my self-confidence by appointing me leader of the band that marched around the room to the beat of little drums and the old upright piano.

To lose my father's presence at home took a lot of fun out of everything for me—even out of my playing with the electric train Santa Claus had brought me one special Christmas. Dad had laid out the track all over the attic. With his own skilled hands he had made the control panel and an accurately scaled freight depot and passenger station. He was a perfectionist, and I bragged to my playmates that he could build anything. But when his Walton Investment Company failed after the 1929 crash, he couldn't seem to rebuild his life, though he tried hard. He started a wood yard business to supply fuel for the black community. He worked out a plan to clear a piece of property in Arkansas for the landowner for a percentage of the cordwood. He then transported his share of the wood to Memphis, where it was cut into stove lengths.

In the summers he sent me over to Arkansas to tally our "credit" for the wood as it was cut, only to hurry me back to Memphis to check in the load when it arrived. Each night I helped my father stack the cut lengths for sale to vendors who later resold it on the street.

One night during a rainstorm we were struggling to move a large loaded wagon away from the saw up a hill to the racks.

About halfway up, a rear wheel dropped into a hole, turning the wagon over on the side where I was pushing. The wagon and cordwood pinned me down in the mud and water. Instantly, my good friend Joe, a muscular black man who always watched over me in the Arkansas forest, leaped into action. With sheer brute strength, he lifted the wagon—wood and all—off a very wet, and very scared "Little Boss"—his nickname for me.

Back home during those months, I sensed, young as I

was, that my father's situation was getting more desperate. At night I could overhear him and my mother talking. He would say to her, "Now, Buddy, I'm going to make it somehow." But things went from bad to worse.

My father's social drinking began to get out of control. Life at home became hectic. Quarrels between our parents got so violent that my little sister and brother and I would run outside and hide in the crawl space under the back porch. The neighbors were talking about us, too. They were even telling their children not to play with us, because the Waltons were going to lose their home and move away.

I was too young to understand the accelerating catastrophe. Then, suddenly, I was jolted into the hard reality of our misfortune.

One dismal day in 1932 we lost our house to foreclosure and had nowhere to go. I could not understand how anyone could take our home. It was ours. On the dark day we were to move out, I ran off and hid in one of the clubhouses I had built.

When my father found me I shouted at him, "This is mine! They can't take this!" I hung on to the shaky little structure, refusing to leave.

Father stepped back, releasing his grip on me. In that particular tone of voice that I always knew meant business, he said, "You, Billy! Straighten up and walk out of there. Right now!"

I bit down on my lip so hard that blood flowed. (Later my grandmother spoke harshly to my father about it, thinking that he had hit me.) But I walked out . . . and away from a happy childhood.

There was no way I could have even imagined then, at age twelve, how similar my situation would be nearly fifty years later when my business fortunes came to a disillusioning and destructive climax. "This is mine!" I wanted to shout again then. "They can't take this!" But they could and they did.

The little frame house we moved to from Linden Avenue was rental property belonging to an in-law branch of our family, who let us have it rent-free. It was in a far less attractive neighborhood, definitely the backyard of nicer things. There was no central heat but rather two heating stoves called "Chill Chasers." My parents took the one bedroom, while my grandmother, whom I called "Mama," slept on the enclosed porch with us three children. The kitchen had no cooking stove, and we had not brought the one from Linden, so for the first few days we ate porridge cooked on a little electric hotplate.

In my shame over our move, I had burst out angrily to my father: "I'll never do this to my little boy!" The words must have been like a knife in his heart, already hurt far beyond my understanding. He was a man who had been proud of his professional achievements, of his good private school education, and of his distinguished forbears—one of whom, Captain William Walton, was a founding patriarch of the Tennessee territory in the 1700s, and the namesake of the Walton Road, U.S. 70 North as it is known today.

With increasing frequency my father came home intoxicated and unaccountable for his actions. Under those conditions I simply had to find a job to help out. I started delivering newspapers, just mornings at first but shortly in the afternoons as well, on a route that required me to get up at 2:30 A.M. and to go out again immediately after school each day. My attitude was a whole lot more serious than it had been in some earlier childish business ventures back on Linden.

They had been more for fun than anything else. Like a lot of kids in every generation, when I was about nine years old I set up a pop stand in the front yard of our red brick bungalow—a "service industry" for those typically humid midsummer days in Memphis. The few pennies it brought in failed to satisfy me.

It was then I hammered out my first expansion plan through franchising. That fundamental business principle would someday call for my most intense concentration as I administered the worldwide expansion of the Holiday Inn system. Back in the twenties, of course, I didn't even know the word "franchise," but an instinct must have been guiding me.

By coaxing and bullying, I recruited a ragtag bunch of neighborhood boys and girls, both older and younger ones, to be my district representatives. From the Walton house, a whole caravan of baby carriages, commandeered from family attics and basements nearby, careened out to the surrounding blocks, sometimes negotiating sharp corners and fire hydrant obstacles on two wheels.

Each of these mobile units contained not a gurgling infant but a sloshing tub full of soda pop to quench the thirst of Memphis mothers and their offspring. Trade thrived, especially at the funeral parlor on Union Street when mourners were coming and going.

For each drink sold, I drained off a one-cent commission. There was a funny thing, though, about those pushers of the bubbly buggies. They were willing enough to work for me, but seldom would they play with me. Some of them even began calling me "Boss Crump," and they would run inside and slam the doors when I wandered down the street looking for a friend.

It wasn't to be the last time in my life that I got that kind of treatment. Decades later it almost proved to be my personal undoing. When nobody from the company's management level will come over to sit with a senior officer at his table in the executive dining room, you can just bet that his problem isn't as simple as bad breath! That solitary man, shunned by his associates, is branded "untouchable" as surely as if he had the mark of Cain seared across his forehead.

Day after day at Holiday Inns headquarters, mocked by my years of leadership laurels, I sat alone and fed on my fury. Though I now wore the title of vice chairman of the board, I had been excommunicated from the inner sanctum of power. Confrontations, jealousy, back-stabbing, and competing egos spread their cancer through the fourth-floor executive suite at Holiday City in Memphis, eating away at corporate integrity. While the brilliant neon star on the Great Sign outside the Inn on Lamar Avenue continued to beckon weary travelers with its promise of hospitality, for me it had become a danger signal. Every trip to the office aggravated my frustrations and fears.

People in business know what I'm talking about. Mole hill disagreements turn into Himalayas of hostility because some piece of turf is threatened, or a pet scheme is thwarted, or an ulterior private motive is exposed. Men and women with imposing titles and impressive positions shut themselves into corporate boardrooms all over America and scrap like alley cats. It's depressing.

Oh, that's not the whole picture, of course. There are other boardrooms where everybody purrs pleasantly while they stroke each other's vanity and skillfully conceal claw and fang by voting yes on whatever proposals are favored by top executives. That's depressing, too, only more so. A fierce fight can sometimes be damaging, but a fixed fight is always sickening.

Don't get the idea that I'm bad-mouthing the free enterprise system or American corporate structure. I believe in both with all my heart. I admit that becoming chairman of the board of the largest hotel operation in the history of the human race was the enticing goal of my business career. When I lost my crack at it, I got mad as blazes at everybody—including God.

I was being set up for all of that back there in those Depression years when other kids resented me. Maybe my entrepreneurship did get a little pushy and high-handed at times.

I'm not saying they had no reason to shut me out of their lives. But whatever justification might have existed, the cold-shoulder treatment started a thirst in me that no baby-carriage fizz-water could slake—a craving to be accepted, to be an insider, to be "one of the gang."

Off and on, I tried some other modestly successful ventures. With my inherited knack for handling a saw and hammer as early as the age of seven, I built clubhouses for kids in neighbors' backyards—for a fee, of course. With some old 2' x 3' signs donated by the Coca Cola Company, I even manufactured some three-piece prefab pop stands, which I sold to my friends to set up in their own yards.

At least once I built a creditable roller-coaster track that zoomed scarily down from a garage roof and across a lawn.

But all of that was left behind after we moved to the other house, which only made our new circumstances that much more puzzling to me. I remember one of the first nights there, sitting beside my grandmother on the edge of the bed on the sleeping porch and asking her, "Mama, why is God letting this happen to us? Have we been bad and done something to make him mad?"

In all of our trouble, I don't recall that my parents ever turned to anyone for help, even a minister. As a family, we were just "pew warmer" church members. But Grandmother knew God, and told me that he loved me.

I can't remember all the details of that lonely, hurting night on the porch, when we had the first of many long talks about God and the one she called "his Son, Jesus." But one thing she said made a lasting impression because it sounded so strange to me.

"Billy," Mama said, "God has a plan for your life, and this is part of the plan. You just trust him."

How could God have a plan for a twelve-year-old boy, I wondered. He might love me, as she said, because they told us in Sunday school that he loved everybody in the world. But, a plan? For me? Well, if Mama said it, it must be true. She could be believed.

Before long, though, there was another very different kind of nighttime conversation. I overheard my father say to Mother, "There just isn't anything here for me. My life is ended here. I must leave and start over again."

A few days later, he sat me down on the back steps of the house, and said, "Billy, straighten up, son. I want to talk to you."

I don't remember all he said. But there's still the echo in my mind of his announcement that he was going to leave, and that he did not know when he would be back, and that I would have to be the man of the house.

"Look after your mother, and your brother and sister. And listen to Maw." (That was his nickname for my grandmother, who he dearly loved, even though she was his mother-in-law. I can still picture them sitting together early in the mornings, drinking coffee and chatting. She loved my father and never seemed to change that attitude even as he became difficult to love in those last days.)

That night, my father packed his things in the little black Ford Model A, a secondhand car he had bought when he sold the other two. Early the next morning, we all had breakfast together. He said good-bye to all of us. I started to cry. "Straighten up, son," was all he said.

He got in the car and drove away, never to return. I can't describe how I felt as I watched that car move out of sight down the street. Often at night I had sat and watched father working terribly hard to get it into good shape. But I checked my tears by remembering that I was the man of the house now, and that sister Betty and brother Van were right there watching me. They were too young to know what was happening; they thought Dad was just taking a trip.

Mother and Mama walked back into the house.

"Katherine, what will you do now?" my Grandmother asked.

"I am going to Colonel Bacon and see if he will send me to Boss Crump. Maybe he can get me a job."

I held my emotions together until I could slip around to the back of the house and hide in the coal shed. Then I cried uncontrollably for a long time, stomping the ground, and pounding my fists in the dirt. My feelings were a snarl of hurt, fear, lostness, and rejection. Never in my wildest imagination could I have guessed this would be only the first of many such times in my life.

For years to come I would feel cheated whenever I saw other boys with their dads. But that morning I hurt too badly to think.

2 ★ Little Boss Starts Climbing

That night we held a family meeting, the first of
regular ones that would continue for the next ten
years, huddled around the old round oak dinner table,
deciding what to do next and desperately cherishing
each other's company.

In her utter humiliation, "Kackie," my mother, went
out the next day as planned, job-hunting for the first
time in her life. Out of my love for her, I felt an
indescribable ache. She did call on Mr. Crump, who got
her a position as a social worker handling needy WPA
family cases.

My all-important newspaper delivery job was with
Mr. Scott, who covered the largest paper route in
Memphis, delivering the *Commercial Appeal* every
morning with a horse and buggy. Standing beside each
other in the bouncing wagon, he threw one side of the
street while I threw the other.

Getting up each morning about 2:30, I walked the
eight blocks to the stable. I stuck to the middle of the
street, whistling, and looking over my shoulder to see if
anyone was following me. At that time of the morning,
it was a world that I had all to myself.

After we hitched up and started for the paper station

three miles away, I would crawl under the tarpaulin in the back of the wagon and take a quick nap. When we had finished loading up our papers, we would buy a dime bag of day-old doughnuts at the bakery.

Later we would meet the horse-drawn milk delivery wagon. Then both drivers would pull over to the curb, where we would sit with the milkman and share doughnuts and chocolate milk in the quiet, predawn hour.

There was one other part to my middle-of-the-street walks in the morning dark: I would talk with the Lord who Mama told me had a plan for my life. I didn't hear any voice talking back to me, but at least it kept me from being totally scared. Come to think of it, an audible reply to my prayers in that setting probably would have turned me into a cross-country runner!

I added a second paper route of my own, for the *Memphis Evening Appeal*, which earned me a pretty respectable combined income. That gave me a chance to do something nice for my mother that was totally unexpected.

One day on my way to pick up my afternoon papers for delivery, I passed a little repair shop a man was operating in his garage. His specialty was rebuilding gas cook stoves. As I stopped to look in, he was just finishing painting a Weter, exactly like the one we used to have on Linden Street. It looked as good as new. He told me he wanted twenty-five dollars for it.

"But, young man, what are you going to do with a gas cook stove?"

"I'm going to give it to my grandmother who is cooking for us on a hot plate."

"Tell you what I'll do," he said. "Since you seem to be such a fine young man, I'll sell it to you for fifteen dollars."

I hadn't been treated so kindly by anyone for a long time, and my thank-you was genuine. He agreed to let me pay him in three five-dollar installments.

"Where do you live, and how do you plan to get the stove home?"

"I don't know how I'll do it, but I'll figure out something."

"Well," he said, "you come back this afternoon and we'll put it in my old truck over there and take it to your home for you."

By the time we got to the house later that afternoon, the new coat of paint was dry and the stove looked great. Kackie was back from work, and Mama was in the kitchen. I'll never forget how proud I felt when we carried that stove into the house and I saw the happy smiles on the faces of those two women whom I loved so much. Unconsciously, perhaps, I felt that this purchase was a start on our way back to the status we had lost. But there would be a rough route to travel over that difficult road.

Not too long after we moved, my old playmates from Linden Avenue rode over on their bicycles to see me—or rather, to see where I lived. Out of the corner of my eye, I caught the cruel flicker of their contempt. They left soon, and I was not to see them again until we were young adults, because they lived in the Bellevue Junior High area, and I was now in the Fairview district.

Fatherless, I was forced to become an adult at twelve. I had to be partner to my mother Kackie and substitute father for five-year-old Betty and two-year-old Van. The shabby house on a back street shamed my mother, and made me care all the more to see her happy again. Her strain and embarrassment infected me with an obsession to become somebody very important someday. One way or another, I promised myself, the time would come when I would be a true "boss," the top man of a big company.

If I had known the words then, I might have said to anyone who asked me what I wanted to be when I grew up: "a business tycoon . . . a corporate executive."

Coming when it did, therefore, Boss Crump's ambitious endorsement of Billy Walton for eventual Senate membership, although he undoubtedly was being facetious, gave me the shove to start my climb toward that shining mountain peak called *success*.

Neither his scheme, nor my dream, anticipated that I really would make it to the United States Senate some forty years later—not as a senator, but as something of a power broker in my own profession of innkeeping. But that chapter came much later.

There were to be lots of shaky reaches and perilous footholds on the way up. But to a boy of twelve, mountains are meant for climbing. I set my heart on reaching the top—never guessing that the final few feet would pose the most agonizing challenge of my life.

The lower slopes are terribly distant from the summit. Now, more than half a century later, I look back on that dilapidated rental cottage, I hear the echo of Boss Crump's gratuitous words to a hardworking twelve-year-old, and I can identify them as spurs to ambition that made me grit my teeth and start climbing for all I was worth. Nothing, I thought then, would stop my progress. At least, not for long.

Childhood experiences set the course of life. By twelve, without any way of knowing it, I had all my motivational drives in place.

But the hard lessons were just beginning.

3 ★ Lighthouse and Safe Harbor

Without Mama, I don't think I could have survived. Kackie's mother stayed with us from as far back as I can remember. Because we lived in small houses for so many years, she and I shared the same bedroom—the same bed, in fact—through much of my early boyhood.

Mother's casework load kept her away all day and left her weary every night. All of us children knew without a doubt that she loved us as we loved her, but she simply didn't have much time or energy to give us. Grandmother, on the other hand, was always there. Mama was the cozy type—short, plump, dimpled. Her gray hair lay in soft waves, and her bright eyes twinkled behind her steel-rimmed glasses.

As I sort through old snapshots, I see that her cotton stockings sagged a bit around her stocky legs. Now and then a flash of white petticoat peeked below the hem of her customary dark dress. But such minor details never detracted from her genteel neatness. In my memory she is always "dressed up." Her physical appearance gave no clue to the force she exerted in shaping my outlook on life. For all her quiet manner, Grandma held strong convictions. Her father was what we around Tennessee call a Hardshell Baptist. That legacy produces solid beliefs and steady behavior. It gives a person a dependable point of reference, like a lighthouse on a rocky coast, when life gets stormy.

That metaphor had first occurred to me to use in a tribute I made in 1950 at a memorial service for our lifelong family friend, Judge Bacon, who had helped my mother get a job through Mr. Crump after father left. Mama was that lighthouse to me, as she beamed her wisdom from a life fueled by her faith and anchored in the rock of God's Word.

Often neglected by my father in my preschool days while he was busy building his investment company, I suffered extreme pangs of loneliness. Mama comforted me. "Always remember," she'd say, "you've got a friend in God. Jesus will always be with you."

I'm not sure I understood that, or even felt it much then. But the fact that Mama said it made it so. God's presence is a mystery to me still, but I've had plenty of experiences to reassure me that my grandmother told the truth. She went beyond giving me general slogans about God's presence.

"Jesus will help you, if you ask him. But remember, Billy, you must believe that he will help you."

Divine help. We're willing to seek it when we're going under, but slow to credit it when we get on top. Someone has said: "The self-made man usually worships his maker." That must be what a certain young executive in Los Angeles spotted in me years afterward that prompted his challenge to me one day.

Twenty-five hundred people in the meeting room held their breath. The electric tension felt like the lull between lightning jab and thunderclap. At the podium, with all eyes fixed on me, within me my two selves raged a civil war.

The public self fought desperately to save face. As vice chairman of the board of Holiday Inns, Inc., I had just delivered a motivational speech to the Los Angeles Sales and Corporate Executives Association. With the same gusto I had displayed through two decades of platform presentations, I described to those men and women the modern business miracle that had made our company the largest of its kind in the world. It was a "people" story, throbbing with vision, initiative, and determination—essentials for greatness in any enterprise. I loved to tell it.

At the same instant, though, my private self unexpectedly demanded a kind of honesty I feared. Business success had gotten me to believing my own press releases. I was a Very Important Person. After all, the company's Lear jet was always at my command, and wherever I landed, people gave me the red carpet treatment. That kind of thing impresses a lot of folks. It impressed me!

The moral showdown I faced in Los Angeles was triggered during the question period that followed my speech. Everything went fine until a sharp young executive stood up. Six feet tall, good-looking, and wearing an impeccably tailored suit, he challenged me.

"You have emphasized the fact that you are a self-made man," he said, "but I can't help feeling you haven't told us the full story."

How right he was!

In that setting, of course, I quickly recovered my wits and offered some plausible generalization that got me off the hook and let the audience breathe again. But the young man's words jolted memories and feelings that drove me to a tough reappraisal of lots of things—about Holiday Inns and about myself.

I had not told that Los Angeles crowd—or anybody else—the "full story." When the executive issued his challenge to me that day in front of all those people, he broke open a clogged channel that Mama had originally engineered.

But it has taken awhile to bring myself to the point of being willing to go public about it all. I've had to retrace a lot of steps in my climb, but I feel I owe it to all my loved ones and lifelong friends to set the record straight now about the "success saga" of Bill Walton. That includes giving credit to those who helped me along the way.

Probably the most important teaching my grand-mother passed along to me is the hardest of all to accept. I can't count the number of times she told me: "The Lord loves you, Billy."

Someday that truth would become the cornerstone for my philosophy of life. But as a boy not privileged to enjoy the close love of a human father, I didn't have any role model for the love of a heavenly Father. The only father I knew in my first twelve years was a man who was often too busy for me to get near, and ultimately was too troubled for me to approach. Under those circumstances, even the love of God can become vague and abstract—a mere concept.

Providentially, I was spared such emptiness of meaning. In my very early childhood, between the ages of three and six, Mama would take me with her to spend a large part of the summer at her family home in Jackson, Tennessee. If she was my lighthouse, then that old mansion was my harbor.

The place was tremendous. Built initially as a girls' school, it had twelve-foot ceilings, hand-painted by an Italian artist. All the woodwork was solid cherry, and there was a sweeping two-story stairway.

Great-grandfather Bray was a prominent personage as the town postmaster. He and his wife (who died at 100) had twelve children. Some of them never moved away from the house in Jackson. Aunt Mim and her husband lived downstairs, another sister made her home on the third floor for fifty years, and on the second floor was Uncle Curtis.

He was my buddy. Oh, I suppose if there was a "black sheep" in Grandma's family, he probably was it. A bachelor who liked his liquor a little too well, Uncle Curtis never worked at a steady job so far as I knew. He collected antiques. Once he gave me a rare treasure which I still have: a signed letter from George Washington concerning some Continental troop matter.

When I grew up and got busy in my Memphis law practice, I'd still slip away to Jackson and the Bray house. There, Uncle Curtis and I—he, the boy who never grew up, and I, the man who had never known full boyhood—would hike together down the many tracks in that important railroad junction. We would stop in at the old hotel and sit for awhile listening to the train men spin their tales. Then we would amble over to the hobo jungle at the edge of town where perpetually wandering tramps drank potent coffee out of battered tin cans.

Sometimes, he and I would even hop a freight, bumming a caboose ride on the GM&O up to Sikeston, Missouri, and then bum our way back again.

There was sweetness and gentleness in that Bray home, exactly the traits that marked Mama. In memory, I still can smell the fragrant cakes and pies ranged on the dining room sideboard. I remember the generous uncle who took me down to the furniture store and bought me my first velocipede.

Mostly, though, I remember that no one who lived there ever said an unkind word about anything or anyone. The pureness of that kind of love is bound to come through if we let it. I soaked it up even if I couldn't define it.

Sometimes I used to ask my grandmother to explain to me the difference between God and Jesus. She tried, but usually ended up by saying, "You'll understand it later, Billy." That was true about love, too.

It is later now, much later. There still are many unanswered questions. But I'm sure of one thing: Back then when life directions were being set, the loving God put Mama there to guide me.

And thinking about her does help me to understand Jesus, who must have been a lot like her.

4 ★ Always into Something

Mama couldn't be with me everywhere, however, especially when the toll of our family upheaval showed up where it hurt a preteen child the most—in school. I was so tired all the time that I couldn't stay awake in classes. My job schedule took the hours I should have given to doing my homework.

Elementary school teachers thought I was lazy, or stupid, or both! One of them moved my desk into the cloakroom, where in "solitary confinement" she lectured me on the evil of my ways. But a more sympathetic Miss Payne said, "He's not really bad—just always seems to be doing something."

It didn't help my case any when I leaned out the narrow cloakroom window one day swinging an ink bottle on a piece of string. The principal chose that very moment to lean out his own window one floor below. In my frantic haste to retract the bottle, I whacked it against the brick wall and spattered the ink all over the man's head!

Not surprisingly, I was expelled from that school eventually, and then from another, unable to give a satisfactory performance as a pupil or a convincing explanation for my misdemeanors.

When the time came at last to register at Fairview Junior High, you can be sure I dreaded it. As the new boy from a different grammar school district, I didn't know any of the other kids. My sense of loneliness grew.

At that dangerous teen age, in the emotional limbo between child and adult, my restless desire to be accepted as one of the group surged. This led me to the threshold of danger with a gang of wild boys and girls doing things that ran counter to everything I'd been taught to respect. For a short while I tried very hard to fit in with them.

Two things saved me from the disasters that ultimately caught up with some of those young people in their escapades. I remembered what Mama had said to me once: "Billy, you have got a good name. You can keep it that way with God's help. That's all you need to go where you want to."

In addition to that wisdom, I was doggedly determined to make something of myself to compensate for what I saw as my father's failures and to make my mother happy.

So, I dropped out of the gang. For the balance of my time in junior high school, I was a loner. That didn't make too much difference anyway, because I was still delivering papers or collecting on my route every afternoon after school, and still helping on the morning route.

At home I tried my best to encourage my dear mother and to be a father-figure for the younger ones. My status there got a little boost when I'd do things like building a doll house for Betty or reconditioning a salvaged bicycle for Van. But the family situation made its mark on my sensitive little sister, so Kackie made arrangements to take her out of public school and enroll her with Miss Loomis in St. Mary's School for Girls.

The summer of 1935, before I entered high school, brought me one of the greatest satisfactions I have ever known. Our economic situation had begun to improve, with Kackie and me both working, and with my father sending back a little money from time to time, which he earned on the Alcan highway construction job he had gotten in Alaska. I was able to replace my afternoon delivery route with a better-paying job in the Liberty Cash Grocery Store after school each day and on Saturdays.

But in the eyes of Memphis society, the Waltons still lived on the wrong side of the tracks. My passionate intention to move back to the Linden Avenue area had not wavered a fraction during the years we had been away.

On an impulse one day I decided to go over and look around the old neighborhood. To my great surprise, a fine house had just been made available to rent at 193 Idlewild, around the corner from 1744 Linden. In my boyish thinking, it seemed unbelievably perfect.

Apparently I made a pretty good case for our moving there when we had our family conference that night around the old oak dining table. The vote in favor was unanimous. We wasted no time in getting our few things together and relocating. I felt that move set things back right again. We were still renters, but in a house of our own choice—and, best of all, back in the neighborhood where we belonged.

What I could not realize then, of course, was that it planted in me what would become a constant obsession to see those I loved situated in comfortable and attractive surroundings. In fact, it may even have been the seed that years later would blossom in my dedication to the comfortable, attractive housing of travelers all over the world through our Holiday Inns system. The trauma of once losing our home made it matter supremely to me that nobody else, if I could help it, would ever suffer that fate.

Just a shadow of disappointment grazed my happiness when I found out that most of my former friends had moved away from that old neighborhood. But at least I was back there. And since I would be entering high

school in the fall, I had to make some new friends
anyway.

To help me in this I enlisted my cousin, Jane Bray.
Older than I by several years, she was a beauty contest
winner, president of her sorority, and an all-around
popular person. She agreed to put in a good word with
Palmer Miller, president of TKO, the boys' high school
fraternity.

I was so buoyed up by our successful escape from the
little cottage of our recent past that I determined to
press for membership. Palmer was agreeable. After all,
I was a cousin of *the* Jane Bray, so who could object?

Everybody, that's who! The move into the nice house
in the nice neighborhood wasn't enough to commend
me, for one reason. Somebody found out about my
short stint in the wild gang at Fairview, and I was
blackballed from the fraternity.

I was totally crushed. Acceptance meant everything
to me. After Palmer called me with the bad news, I
went out into the backyard, kicking the dirt and crying,
"God! Can't you help me—just once? Mama said you
would. I want to get into that fraternity. I like those
fellows and I want to join them. Please!"

I like to think that God chose to overlook my anger
and to listen to my anguish instead. A little later that
same night, Palmer called me again. He'd hit on a plan.

"Billy," he said, "the problem is that those fellows
don't know you as well as I do. When they do, they'll be
glad to take you in. You come along with me as my guest
to the next several meetings so that you will really get
to know them, too. Then I will ask them to vote again."

The plan worked. The next time my name was
brought up for membership, I passed with no difficulty.

It turned out to be no insignificant adolescent
triumph. Friendships I made in the fraternity have
lasted to this day—wonderful people who were to affect
the very course of my life in many ways. Relationships
between young people are not trivial and need not be
temporary. I'm grateful that the Father in heaven who
was lovingly watching over me got me into the right

crowd just when I needed it so desperately. I could wish as much for everybody's children.

It is true that at first I was a little uneasy as to how my new friends might react to my working in a grocery store. But one of the fraternity leaders soon laid that anxiety to rest when he said reassuringly, "Billy, remember that I work in my uncle's hardware store."

It didn't hurt my ego or my image a bit, either, when a pretty girl (who was to be involved in my life for the next seven years) would drive up in front of Mr. Montesi's store to pick me up in her swanky LaSalle automobile! Such things did more to encourage me and to bolster my self-respect than anybody could guess.

That girl, and two others during those years, had a favorable influence on my life. Teenage crushes may be ridiculed by adults with short memories, but there may be no other time in a person's life when it is more crucial to be liked for who you are as an individual. The psychological bruises of my boyhood did not heal speedily, and I owe a lot to those patient and caring high-school friends.

I had one other morale booster. That same fall of 1935, Kackie and I were able to buy a used 1929 Model A Ford, and I started to drive. This turned out to be a major factor in my fraternity life. Whenever my TKO brothers threw a party, their parents would let them borrow the family car only if Billy Walton went along to drive.

While that pleased the anxious moms and dads, it didn't always win me points with the boys. Some of them thought I was a wet blanket because I could always spot trouble coming and give them a lecture of caution. I suspected that they used me sometimes without truly liking me, but I gladly put up with that slight discomfort just for the privilege of being included in their activities. We all survived the era without wrecks or injuries.

My dating life flourished, too. I went sometimes to the Memphis Country Club for Sunday night dinner and show with the daughter of one of our most prominent physicians. When he would come home and find my '29 Ford parked in his driveway, he would jokingly ask his daughter whose "bunch of junk" was blocking his Cadillac. He would sometimes talk with me about my views on some of the current happenings in Memphis, as though he really was interested in my opinion.

The parents of my "steady" girl gave her a maroon Buick convertible just about the time Kackie and I were able to buy a new car for the first time, a 1937 Ford. In more ways than one, I was riding high. She was a Princess in the Cotton Carnival, and I was one of her Princes. She was Queen of our fraternity, and I was vice president. Her father told her: "That young man is going somewhere." He didn't say where, but I'll always think of him with affection because he was the first person of his stature to say such a thing. He was probably the first adult man I considered to be my friend, other than Uncle Curtis.

My cousin Jane and friend Palmer taught me to dance and to behave with the proper social graces. Every June and Christmas each fraternity gave a dance, making a total of eighteen—and I went to every one!

Sometimes that created complications. One time I didn't have time to go home afterwards and change clothes before school started. I arrived at geometry class in my dress shirt, tuxedo pants, and shiny shoes. "Did you have a good time last night, Billy?" asked Miss Steward, and went right on with her class lecture. I considered her a good friend. She tried awfully hard to teach me geometry!

Then there was Kitty Bright—undisputed as the most beautiful, blue-eyed blonde in Central High School and a straight-A honor student. We had homeroom together, and she would always hear my name read out on one of "those lists" I dreaded.

"Billy," she would say to me, "why don't you study more and improve your grades?" We dated occasionally, even though she had a "steady" and so did I. We were good friends. But my grades didn't improve.

The high-school years were fulfilling in many other

ways, though. I was elected an officer of the fraternity, captain of Company "C" of the Central ROTC, and—for a very short time—a member of the football team.

That winning team was the school's pride and joy, and it would make my career complete, I thought. Coach Mogevney took one look at me and said, "Red, you are too small."

"Coach, I'm fast though. Just let me try."

"OK, but you be careful. Stay out of the way of some of those big fellows. I'm afraid you'll get hurt."

It was hard to find a football uniform that didn't completely swallow me, but I finally got suited and lumbered out to the practice field. I had never realized those fellows I saw in class every day could look so big in uniform!

Coach would put me into a play and tell the defending team, "Now y'all protect Red. Don't let him get hurt."

They would block their hearts out protecting me. Or trying to. I was fast all right, but not fast enough. Finally, after they had dug me out of the mud a few times and gotten the breath back into me, Coach decided he better whisk me out of there, thus ending my athletic career.

ROTC was better suited to my size and ability. Under my captaincy, our unit won honors in city-wide competition. All I had to do was present my company for inspection review and then march in the big parade with my girlfriend at my side and silver saber flashing in the sun. It sure beat getting tackled!

In all these ways I was gaining much-needed self-confidence and strengthening my determination to make something more of myself than just a campus VIG (Very Important Guy). At last my big chance came to make a political reputation, and perhaps to start moving toward the U.S. Senate as Boss Crump had prophesied.

But it almost backfired on me!

A good friend of mine who was running for student government president enlisted me as his campaign manager. The entrepreneurial flair that went back to my baby carriage pop-running days flourished anew. As the crucial election approached, I borrowed a sound truck with the help of my old friends at the Coca Cola Company, wangled a supply of candy kisses from Sears Roebuck to bribe voters, and rounded up some genuine soapboxes for the speechmakers.

On the fateful day, the whole grand design came together in a political rally in front of the school—at 7:00 in the morning!

Sound truck, candy, banners, balloons, soapbox speeches, and "cheering throngs" of high-schoolers. It was perfect!

Except—directly across the street, a prominent Memphis minister was shocked awake by the pre-breakfast bedlam and promptly called the newspaper. The *Press-Scimitar* dispatched a photographer on the instant, and the story appearing later that day reported a "riot" in front of Central High School, complete with front-page pictures of the "disgraceful conduct."

I was called to the principal's office, where I was told I had embarrassed the school and might be expelled. History was repeating itself!

I got a chance later that day to explain the whole thing to a reporter from the morning paper. So, the next day, the *Commercial Appeal* presented the event in a totally different light. It praised us innovative young people for a stimulating demonstration of the democratic process: "One of the finest examples of the great American tradition of campaigning for a candidate in an election on a high school campus ever seen in Memphis."

Immediately I was a hero. The principal said, "Billy, I was a little hasty."

Outside of my hectic school schedule (more social than scholarly), I found time for two other all-important steps in my life. One was joining the Idlewild Presbyterian Church.

Every Sunday morning at 11:00 in the main sanctuary I served as an usher. There were older folks who questioned why "that boy" was given such an important assignment, but the elder in charge of the ushering wanted me to stay, and he even let me serve on many Sunday afternoons when the choir would give a recital. I took my duties seriously and did my best. But I didn't necessarily like everything about my church experience.

I remember coming home from one of the first services and complaining to my Baptist grandmother about the minister. "I'm sure he's a great man and well educated," I said, "but why must he pray as if his prayers were an oration? Why can't he just talk to God? Isn't that what God wants us to do? That's what you told me to do, Mama. Am I wrong?"

"Billy," she said, in her usual gentle way, "just remember that God loves you and cares about you. Talk to him as your Father. He is always with you."

I wanted God to be proud of me, and I was really ashamed about my poor grades in school.

"Are you sure," I would ask Mama, "that God knows every little thing we do, and all about us all the time?"

She assured me he did. It didn't cheer me up.

But I took my religion very seriously. I thought that if I was good, didn't drink or smoke, and did good works, my place in heaven was a sure thing. Still, this was not the controlling motivation of my life.

Instead, what haunted me constantly was the drive to better our family position in society. Then, about halfway through the eleventh grade, that dream was momentarily threatened.

We had settled comfortably into the rented house on Idlewild and had fixed it up nicely to suit us. Without warning, the owner gave us notice that he had sold the house to an architect who wanted possession in thirty days.

Back at the old oak dining table in a family conference, it was decided that I should go out the next day and try to find us a new home. Since we were already established once more in a nice neighborhood, that wasn't the issue it had been before. So I was free simply to go looking for a suitable house.

I found one I liked almost immediately—such a great house in my eyes, in fact, that I was afraid to inquire about it. I dredged up enough courage, though, and learned its sale was being handled by E. H. Crump and Company.

When I reported my findings to the family that night, Kackie said she knew the agent in charge and would call him the next day.

He turned out to be the proverbial friend in need. "Katherine," he told her, "that piece of property is probably the best buy we have. It was foreclosed during the Depression and taken over by Metropolitan. You can buy that house for $5,000 with just $200 down, because they are eager to decrease the number of foreclosure properties they have on their books."

The family conference at the oak table that night was animated indeed! The house was a wonderful bargain, and just what we wanted. But $200! An impossible amount in our circumstances.

Nevertheless, we went ahead and contacted the bank for a loan. They turned us down. (Years later, I would find myself in the position of personally owing that same bank $1,300,000 on ninety-day notes!) We decided to go to Jackson, Tennessee, to see if Uncle John Langston would lend us the money. It was a wonderful return to the fertile ground where our family roots went so deep among loving people. Uncle John agreed the house was a good buy and promptly loaned us the needed money.

With only a few days left before we had to vacate our house, the real estate agent brought us the contract and we closed the sale. My sense of importance knew no limits when I was told it was necessary for me to sign all the papers. For the first time since my father's financial reversal, we owned our own home—111 North Belvedere—where we would spend many happy years until we sold it in 1947.

Then came the blow that devastated my dreams.

Graduation time was drawing near, and excitement was mounting at Central High. In each homeroom, the lists of names of the graduating class were read out.

The name of Billy Walton was not called.

Kitty Bright turned around in her seat and looked at me, tears brimming in her beautiful blue eyes.

"Billy, I'm so sorry."

I was totally humiliated. It seemed I was one-half point short of the required credits. No matter how I pleaded and argued my case, I was told that rules were rules and no exceptions could be made.

I actually ran out of the building, through the alley behind the school, and under the football stadium where I cried until I was drained dry. This time I was really alone. God had forgotten me. Why? Just half a point!

I waited until almost dark before starting home, staying in the alley almost all the way. I tried to slip into the house unnoticed. Mama was waiting for me.

"Billy! Where have you been? I've been worried about you." She looked at me in a way that only a best friend can, and said, "Tell me what's wrong."

We sat down and I told her.

"This time, Mama, I know God has forgotten me." I poured out my story. She listened until I finished, and then told me what I needed to hear.

"Now, Billy, you shouldn't blame God for your lack of discipline. You know that you have been going out every night and not getting your lessons done. Your problem is not God's fault. It would be wrong for him to answer a prayer when you have been so neglectful. God wants you to learn to discipline yourself so that he can use you as his friend someday."

How could an eighteen-year-old high school boy understand what his grandmother was saying about God finding use for him? Yet there was that lighthouse of her faith shining its steady beam once again into my darkness. I knew she was right, even if I didn't know the meaning of her words.

"Billy," she said, "you must trust God with your life and be obedient. Don't question him. He has a plan."

A plan? In the face of crushing disaster, how could that be possible?

By the time Kackie came home from work, I had gotten myself together so that we could talk about my problem as one hurt buddy to another. I told her how sorry I was. She helped me revive my determination to face the next few days, and the weeks and months beyond.

"What? Billy Walton not graduating!" I could imagine everyone saying this. But my friends were considerate of my feelings and treated me with tenderness. It was a lesson I never forgot.

Commencement Day came. I went downtown, alone, to the auditorium where the exercises were held. In the last row of the upper balcony, I watched my best friends graduate—the Class of '38.

Later that evening I joined them as they celebrated and then saw them safely home—as usual. As I returned to our house, I raised just a small question: "Will I ever amount to anything at all? Does God really have a plan?"

In the double darkness of that night, I sincerely prayed for him to show me the way. I knew what lay ahead: my friends going off to college, while I went back to Central High for the short time necessary to earn the single point to get my diploma.

Through the intervening summer, I worked full time in the grocery store while my friends excitedly discussed their college plans. I was beginning to save some money, with the dream of going to Vanderbilt Law School. When the long summer ended, I saw my friends off at the train, put my pride in my pocket, and went back to Central High.

During the last months of 1938 after my return to school, I took on the official role of Big Brother, since I wasn't really a "high school man" anyway. Shortly after we moved into the house on Belvedere I got some of my TKO fraternity brothers to help me convert a large area in the basement into a room suitable for our business meetings and an occasional party. It was like

the early days on Linden when I had built clubhouses
for the kids. Thus our home became a center of activity
for "The Fellows"—my closest personal friends, as well
as for all the fraternity members.

Christmas of '38 at the Waltons' was a great time,
with the family together in our own house, and my
friends coming and going for holiday festivities. The
only cloud on the horizon was the antics of a strange
little paperhanger in Europe named Adolf Hitler, but
there was an ocean stretching safely between us and
the ills of the rest of the world, so why should we
worry?

We would worry soon enough.

Finally, on January 20, 1939, the coveted certificate
from Central High School came to hand. Today, as I
read the solemnly official words inscribed on the
yellowing diploma, I wonder what my teachers really
might have thought in place of this: "He leaves the
school with the respect and confidence of the Board
and Instructors, and their best wishes for his success."

Was there anyone there, I wonder now, who actually
expected the Walton boy to achieve anything
important?

Professor Jester did manage to find a kind word for
me as he handed me the diploma: "You know, Billy, I
am going to miss you each year as we have the student
government elections. I will always remember who
started the political campaigns."

The disgrace of not finishing with my class was offset
a little by two extravaganzas I engineered in connection
with my fraternity life. The first had been a June dance
for TKO, the largest party ever given by a high school
fraternity.

During the years, those dances had always been very
exclusive affairs, with no more than two or three
hundred invitations, just enough to fill the ballroom at
the Peabody Hotel or a country club. It bothered me,
the boy who always was seeking acceptance for
himself, that so many wonderful girls and fellows were
left out of the parties.

My plan was to rent the North Hall of the Auditorium, Memphis' largest gathering place. We would send 1,000 invitations to a gala that would make history!

But how do you decorate a cavernous room large enough to accommodate the Ringling Brothers Circus? The eager high school group working with me was undaunted. Using white wooden arbors, a stage gazebo for the band, and spring flowers and foliage, we transformed North Hall into a garden of vining red roses.

To add to the spectacular atmosphere, we borrowed a damaged parachute from the local National Guard and suspended it upside down from the ceiling. Inside it we stored hundreds of inflated balloons and "confetti" of punchings from notebook paper which a local printer gladly donated. At the appropriate moment, in the split second between the crowning of the Dance Queen and the striking up of the Grand March by the band, we tipped the parachute and showered the room with a rainbow of balloons and the little round bits of paper. My first major event was a blockbuster success!

Nothing succeeds like success, they say. So Billy Walton was next put in charge of planning for a national TKO convention in Memphis late in 1939. By now graduated from Central High, I could devote all my spare time outside of working hours at the store to mastermind another historic event.

As a matter of fact, it turned out to be as big a national meeting as Memphis had ever hosted up to that time. Complete with a Queen's Court full of pretty princesses from the various sororities, mass sessions typical of political conventions, banquets, and general election hoopla, the TKO happening got front-page coverage in the newspapers. More than two hundred delegates from thirty-five chapters in eleven states put Memphis on the map of the national high school social scene. And the once blackballed social outcast, Billy Walton, was chairman of the convention!

Still, in spite of the momentary glory of such achievements, I flinched at the challenge of getting into college. The school records blatantly showed that I had never learned to study properly.

But Boss Crump had once told me I'd have to be a lawyer before I could be a senator, so my sights were set on law school.

It's hard to go into the world at eighteen not knowing for sure if anybody really believes in you—except yourself and your family. And it wouldn't take me long to find out again that very few people were likely to give me a boost up that success mountain. The climb was going to summon my own maximum effort for the next forty years.

If I could have seen everything that was coming, I might have settled for staying a stock boy at Liberty Cash Grocery Store!

5 ⋆ An Entrepreneur Is Born

It looked as if I might be on the verge of breaking away after all. I wasn't quite so foolish as to think I could get into Harvard, or some such fancy place. But I did allow myself the fantasy of graduating someday from Vanderbilt. How I ached to go there!

To play it safe, though, I sent off applications to several schools. It soon became clear that I was still dreadfully close to the bottom slope of that mountain I had started to climb at twelve.

Nevertheless, through some unexplainable generosity on their part, the officials at Ole Miss accepted my application. Soon I began to get rush letters from fraternities on that campus who had apparently heard of my TKO exploits.

Then I found out that behind Kackie's enthusiastic encouragement that I go away to college was her plan to take a second mortgage on the Belvedere house. I knew she could not possibly afford those extra payments without seriously affecting the entire family, and I loved her more than ever for being willing to make the effort. There was no way I could tolerate the thought that we might be forced into foreclosure a second time.

"Kackie," I said, "I have an idea. Memphis State College has great pre-med and pre-law courses. I can get my pre-law there, and then transfer to Vanderbilt Law School."

She may have been even less in favor of that idea than I was, but we agreed to it. What else could we do? Even so, the added financial burden of college costs posed a problem for us. My mother urged me to call one of our relatives, Dr. Ernest Ball, who was then superintendent of Memphis city schools, for help in getting me some type of work scholarship at Memphis State.

"Billy," Dr. Ball told me, "you can get an education almost anywhere if you really want one. Remember, Lincoln got his in front of the log fire in his cabin at night. Certainly you can take your pre-law program at Memphis State."

As for the job? "Sure," he said, "I can get you a National Youth Administration job."

Confidently, I went to see Dean Robinson at the college. "Yes," he greeted me, "I have been expecting you."

I assumed that because cousin Ernest had made his call, using his clout in the city school system, naturally the dean would give me the red carpet treatment. I was grateful, of course, but not exactly thrilled at the prospect of continuing the exhausting pattern that had held me back for years: work hard as much as possible, and study whenever I could squeeze it in.

When I found out what my work assignment on campus at Memphis State was to be, though, even my gratitude wavered. They put me to work on grounds maintenance.

Back then, there were no structures in front of the old administration building, but only a sweeping, parklike expanse of grass. On those broad green acres, I was farmed out for mowing and weeding, and what-ever other custodial care might be required.

For a future senator from Belvedere Avenue, the humiliation was almost too much! I, who had pictured myself absorbed with the "weightier matters of the law" in the illustrious archives at Vanderbilt, was stuck in my hometown with a rake in my hand, studying (when possible) the history of civilization and other such exotic required courses in the liberal arts. I hardly viewed the so-called scholarship that had put me into this mess as a blessing.

I took a kind of perverse pleasure, at last, in the fact that Memphis State had only recently become a full-fledged college, after operating as a state teachers' school. While I certainly was not a VIG on this campus as I had been at Central High, there really wasn't that much to be a Very Important Guy in—no football team of much significance, nor any other student activity for that matter.

So, resenting my job, I looked around for something else to do that might compensate my injured pride at least a little bit. A dim basement corridor in the administration building turned out to be my promised land.

The entrepreneur in me rallied to meet Memphis State's lack of a student union facility. There was no spot on campus where one could get cold drinks, sandwiches, candy, or other between-class snacks—no place to lounge around and just shoot the breeze.

I marched into the bursar's office one day to lay out my plan. I proposed to set up a pop stand in the large vacant area just under the massive marble staircase in the Ad building. It was like being twelve years old again—and back to square one.

He liked the idea. There was only one catch. He had no money in the budget for it. If I could put it together without any money, I could go ahead. So, what else is new?

Not to be denied this chance to create a needed service for my fellow students, I contacted my old reliable supply source, the Coca Cola Company, to negotiate for some equipment and startup stock.

I have to say this for the Coke people: they always came through for me. Back around 1930 it was their friendly routeman who gave me some of their

discarded tin signs to make the front and sides of my
prefab pop stand industry. He also got me bottle
openers, ice picks, caps, and other giveaways that
helped stimulate my business.

Then there was that infamous political rally in high
school when they not only let me borrow a sound truck
but also furnished a Coca Cola bar. Many, many years
later I was to turn to them again for crucial help at the
start of my career with Holiday Inns.

For my Memphis State project back there in 1940, they
invited me to their warehouse where I found exactly
what I wanted in old-fashioned ice cream parlor tables
and chairs (which they even painted for me), as well as
a counter and the indispensable cold-drink box.

Encouraged by this generous support from "fellow"
executives at Coca Cola, I went next to the Tom's
Company and prevailed on them to provide display
racks and a stock of candy and cookies.

Gathering more nerve as I went along, I called the
Mrs. Drake Sandwich Company and got a stock of their
products plus display racks. The crowning touch was
when the Hostess Cake Bakery supplied their
cupcakes—and another display rack!

I was in business in a week—allowing time for the
new paint job to dry on my tables and chairs. From the
first day, I had a crowd. Almost right away the enterprise began making money for the school.

Dean Robinson couldn't believe it all happened so
fast, and he was overjoyed to have some money coming
in from such a limited investment (what investment?!).
Cousin Ernest Ball got a good report on me, of course.
And I didn't have to rake leaves anymore.

As the school year drew to a close, Dean Robinson
summoned me to his office. He said he wanted to talk
about next year. My education? No. He wanted to
enlarge the student lounge space, put in some
additional equipment, add some small capital from
school funds, and strike a more advantageous deal for
me. I told him I'd let him know within a week, but I
knew right away I wouldn't be back. (Judging from the

beautiful student union building that eventually evolved on the campus, I could probably have made that refreshment concession my life work!)

But, though I have a big streak of the dreamer in me, I hold a very realistic respect for the facts. They may dictate a course of action I don't like, and even cause me considerable unhappiness, but I have always tried to base my decisions on the evidence.

Looking back to the Memphis State situation, I can only believe that God directed me down the right road even though it seemed then as if I was taking a detour down a dead-end lane.

What happened, you see, was that I didn't go back to Memphis State College the next year at all. At home, Betty and Van were growing up, and their needs were increasing in normal fashion. The cost of our improved standard of living rose faster than Kackie's government income. The time had come for me to become fully employed as a wage earner for the family.

The thought of not finishing my education concerned me a lot, causing some anxious prayers. But my hopes and dreams for personal advancement had to be set aside as long as there were other lives depending on me.

I got work at McKesson Robbins, a wholesale drug firm, as an order-filler on the "sundries and notions" conveyor line. My financial resources skyrocketed. One of my earliest pay stubs shows eight-day earnings, for sixty-four hours of work, of $18.46—with a 19¢ Social Security deduction. Added to Kackie's wages, that helped the Waltons some to keep the wolf from the door, but not enough.

On the job, my instincts for cost-efficient operations came to the surface. I noticed that there were large numbers of back orders coming through. It struck me as a waste of time and money that we order-fillers, working on one of the lower floors of the building, would empty the shelves and wait awhile before stock was replenished from the storage areas on upper floors. I set to work designing a very simple system of inventory control to keep the shelves full at all times. The manager not only thanked me; he installed that system throughout the company.

It was simply too frustrating to me, though, to be getting nowhere with my educational plans. I decided to talk again to cousin Ernest Ball and to my uncle and old friend, Judge Bacon, about a night law school that had come to my attention. Both men agreed it was a very good basic school. After two years of study, I would be qualified to take the bar exam.

Thus, my actual legal education began, with classes from 7:00 to 11:00 five nights a week, and Saturday and Sunday afternoons from 1:00 to 5:00. That was a switch for me. Until then I had spent my life trying to get an education in the daytime and working at night, many times nearly all night. Now, I was working days and going to school nights! Many times I asked myself: Why am I doing this? Why is this activity so important, to the almost total exclusion of all else? And, the biggest question of all: Where will it all lead?

I'm afraid my prayers at that time were inspired more by doubt than faith. "God, how could you possibly have a plan like this for my life? Can't you help me just a little more? Can't you show me just a glimpse of where you are leading me?"

I didn't see how God, with all the important things he had to do, really could care about me or have a plan for me.

"Billy," my grandmother would say to me in those moments when I confided to her my doubts and fears, "that is the devil putting those thoughts into your head, trying to destroy God's plan."

Then I began to wonder if God and I had the same plan for my life at all. "God," I would pray, "I want to do what you want me to do, but I'm just not sure what it is."

Frankly, I often wanted to slack off or give up altogether. But a quality in me that a friend in later years would describe as "bulldog tenacity" kept me straining toward my goal—the top of the mountain—

almost obscured in clouds of bewilderment.

Not being a good student in the first place, and not having much time for homework between night classes and day work, I began to feel again that old sense of aloneness, of rejection, of facing a hopeless situation. Just then, the Lord brought something along to perk up my spirits.

War was accelerating in Europe, and Great Britain contracted with the DuPont Company to build a munitions plant in Millington, Tennessee, just twenty miles north of Memphis. A friend of Kackie's went to work for DuPont in the construction division.

When I learned that salaries were nearly double what I was earning, I asked him if he could get me a job. Almost before I knew what was happening, I left the drug company and went to work for DuPont as a material control expediter in their Chickasaw Ordnance Works. No matter how efficient our builders were, if they did not find the required materials and equipment on hand at the job site exactly when needed, there was no way they could maintain their construction schedule. I could never in this world have guessed how vitally important that job was to me as training for the time when Holiday Inns would operate a building schedule that would permit us to open a new facility on the average of every two and a half days. At one time, we could have in excess of $120 million worth of Holiday Inns under construction.

Figures at DuPont weren't quite that impressive, but my paycheck surely was. For my first two weeks on the job, I earned $49.77, with 50¢ withheld for Social Security.

Now I began to learn in earnest how immensely valuable it is for people to work together to accomplish goals. During those war years, companies with construction contracts that met their schedules received the government's "E Award" ("E" for Excellence). We beat our schedule by many months, and received the "E" in a splendidly impressive ceremony.

When the newly-completed plant was turned over to the DuPont Operations Division, I was offered a job as assistant purchasing agent. I was only twenty-one years old—making me the youngest person in such a position with DuPont. Obviously I had established a good reputation with the company management. But there was something I valued even more—the friendship of those men in the field who were the construction superintendents. Through their dedication I came to appreciate the virtues of honesty and integrity in one's job. I also saw the impact of a company that cared about its employees.

That DuPont attitude directly affected my own self-esteem, which had suffered so many blows in my growing-up years. Even my superior, Mr. Richmond, would ask my opinion on certain matters of business judgment, making me feel that he was interested in me and that I mattered. It is understandable that to this day I still favor purchasing DuPont products whenever I have a choice, knowing that they do not compromise quality.

One day Mr. Richmond called me to his office with big news. The company wanted to transfer me to the Wilmington payroll and send me to Sylacauga, Alabama, to a new plant construction where I would be put in charge of material control and purchasing. I was now twenty-two years old—and the offer bowled me over.

"By the way," he added, "you will be deferred from military service because you will be in a critical national defense occupation."

When I regained my composure, I thanked him and asked for a few days to consider. Transfer to the Wilmington payroll meant a lifetime position with the DuPont Company as long as you did a good job. On the other hand, moving to Alabama would interrupt my law education, which was by now well underway.

Kackie's reaction was predictable. She was happy for me and flattered by my promotion, as was I. Especially, as a mother, she thought my deferment from military service would be "wonderful."

As our family conference around the oak dining table continued far into the night, she at last got around to saying, "Dear, it's a decision you must make. I know you don't want to quit law school when you are so close to finishing. And I have always known how loyal you feel to your country. I will stand with you on any decision you make."

". . . and so will God." That was Mama's voice, entering the discussion for the first time that night.

Another crossroads. If I went with DuPont, I could not finish the law degree—but I would not need a law degree if I went with DuPont. If I did not go with DuPont, I could finish the degree, but I would be subject to the military draft—and then what use would the law degree be?

"God, show me the way. What do you want me to do?"

At that point in my life there was another very special person I could ask for advice. Pat, the girl I had been dating most of the time I had been going to law school, was the oldest daughter of one of Memphis' prominent families. Her father liked me, but her mother thought I would never amount to anything. Pat was a serious-minded, deeply sincere person, who had encouraged me on more than one occasion.

The following Saturday night, at dinner, she listened attentively to my dilemma. When I finished my story, she hesitated only a few seconds before commenting.

"Bill, for as long as I have known you, you have shown strong determination about where you are going. I share your feeling that there is a purpose for your life, and your sense of it is very noticeable. I don't believe you'll ever be happy until you get wherever it is you have set your mind to go. This DuPont development, as wonderful as it is—and I am happy for you—just seemed to happen. It's not part of your plan. I don't think you should vary from your plan."

I remember her words because they were so much like what Mama had always told me. So, that weekend,

I decided to stay with my plan, to finish my education, get the law degree, and apply for my license to practice.

On Monday I went to Mr. Richmond's office and told him my decision. I said I was only six months away from finishing work for my degree. My plan was to practice for a while, then enter politics and run for a seat in the U.S. Senate. (The naivete of my expectations astonishes me now as I think about it.)

"Well!" my supervisor exclaimed, with almost as much amazement as I myself felt at what I had just said. "Son, I must admire your stubborn determination to reach a goal. But I think you are making a mistake. You can stay in your job here with operations as long as you want it. Good luck with your plan."

So I continued to work at DuPont—even though, in later years, it was to become clear that my plan and God's had not been the same. In all, I was there for two and a half years.

On schedule this time, in June of 1941, I graduated with my class, receiving the LLB degree. While it wasn't a "Doctor of Jurisprudence" degree like the college-educated lawyers had, at least I had successfully leaped the first hurdle on the course Boss Crump had pointed out to me nine years earlier. In later years, Memphis State University purchased the night school, Southern Law University, merged it into its own law school, and reissued all our certificates with a Memphis State University Law School degree.

On March 20, 1942, after taking the bar exam, I was granted the license that entitled me "to practice law in all the courts of the State of Tennessee." In a letter a few months later the secretary of the board of law examiners, R. I. Moore, very kindly wrote this endorsement: "He is a young man with very high principles, thoroughly honest and patriotic, of an alert mind, full of energy and industry . . . an all-around fine young man of high standing in this community with the full respect of everyone who knows him."

William B. Walton, Attorney-at-Law—at last!

6 ★ Reporting for Duty

Three weeks after Mr. Moore wrote his letter, I enlisted
in the Air Force. The war situation in Europe had
worsened critically, and the Pearl Harbor attack by the
Japanese on December 7, 1941, had catapulted the U.S.
into the world conflict. When the president reached
into the fishbowl for the draft lottery, he pulled out my
number first.

I could have gone back to Mr. Richmond, accepting
the Sylacauga job and its automatic deferment. But I
felt there were others who could do that job. Besides,
my old high-school "Fellows"—my best friends—had
decided as a VIG group to go downtown together and
enlist in the United States Army Air Force to receive
cadet training to be pilots.

At the Walton family meeting around the oak table,
Kackie was just a little upset when she heard what I
intended to do instead of taking the job promotion/
military deferment package.

Mama said, "Katherine, he will be all right."

There was the usual waiting period to be called. Each
day we watched the mail delivery for our orders.
Toward the end of 1942, when the orders began to
come through, it was immediately obvious that the

VIGs were not going together as hoped. Only four of us "Fellows" were among the large group ordered to report in Nashville on March 11, 1943, for induction and classification.

There are 10,999,999 other GI's who will agree with me that this was an experience never to be forgotten—an understatement if there ever was one! We marched, we stood in line, we waited, we were tested—in more ways than I would have conceived in my wildest nightmares. After getting shots, haircuts, government-issue clothing, and steel helmets (replacing the felt hat I had always been known to wear), we lacked only the goggles, scarves, and leather helmets of the hot pilots in romantic war movies!

Finally we were interviewed by a major in the medical department, a psychiatrist. When my turn came, he started out in a very formal manner.

"Cadet Walton, I have reviewed your file, and I am—" He stopped. Then he went on in a much different tone of voice, respectful and almost confiding, it seemed to me.

"Bill, let me talk to you. You are bound to know that you are older than most of the boys applying for pilot training. They're eighteen, nineteen, twenty. Your record shows that you are inclined to be direct, that you think through a situation, and make firm decisions. You also have a law degree."

He paused. Were they going to start me out with the rank of general?

"From your record, and from my own interview with you, I must tell you that you have the qualities of leadership that the Air Force needs badly in instructors for these young men."

They were young! What about me?

"Bill," he went on, "we have an order to pull out any applicant we find suitable, and put him into CIS— Central Instructors School—for preparation to be an Air Force Instructor Classification Critical 938. I am sorry to disappoint you."

Disappoint! That was hardly the right word for it. I

was all set in my heart to join my best friends "climbing high into the sky . . . off with one helluva roar." Now this psychiatrist was telling me that I was grounded before I even had a chance to try on my goggles!

"Major," I said, "you just don't understand." (Only a green cadet would say that to a major.) "For once in my life, I want to go along with The Fellows."

"I'm sorry," he repeated.

My initial hurt was boiling into anger. "Look," I retorted, "I made a contract with the Air Force to give me pilot training. If you're not even going to give me a crack at it, just send me home!"

"Be reasonable, Bill," he said quietly. "They will just draft you the next day."

Such unassailable logic won out over my emotions, even though I could not believe this was happening to me all over again.

The next few days were painful for us—John May, Marty O'Callahan, Pee Wee Phillips, and "Red" Walton. When the day came for me to be shipped out, John, who was still waiting for his orders, walked to the plane with me. At boarding time, we both just stood there with uncontrolled tears running down our not-so-manly cheeks.

Immediately I was involved in one of the most concentrated and accelerated training programs I could imagine. The major certainly had not overstated the fact that the Air Force was in a hurry. During the next months I got intensive instruction in administration, communication, organization, and basic principles of leadership. There was total orientation to the B-17 bomber: systems, armaments, crew reponsibilities. My job was to teach the operation procedures of the ship, including its armaments and defensive procedures, and to discipline the crew to interact with one another as a team.

After completing my own training at Buckley Field in Fort Myers, Florida, and Lowry Field in Denver, I was ordered to report for duty at the Las Vegas Army Air

Force base. This is where all the pilots, navigators, bombardiers, radio men, crew chiefs, and gunner position men assembled. After we taught them how to defend their ship from enemy attack, we taught them to function as a team.

Who were these ominous-sounding crews? Mostly, they were brave yet scared kids. It's hard to find words to describe the courage of these young American airmen. I had never felt such a heavy burden to do a job right. I never lost sight for one minute of the fact, the stark reality, that we must do everything in our power to give these young men a fighting chance to return to their homes and families.

I knew that the B-17s were then going mostly to the Eighth Air Force, operating from bases in England on daylight raids into western Europe and, ultimately, directly into Germany. Daylight raids really left our aircraft vulnerable to all the ground fire the enemy could throw at them. The American policy was "precision bombing," using the famous Norden bombsight, so that we could practically aim a bomb right down the smokestack of a factory. The British, on the other hand, did saturation bombing at night, letting their loads of destruction fall in patterns over wide-ranged targets.

I also knew that for the longest leg of their flights, the B-17s would be without fighter escorts. Their chance of survival was going to depend almost entirely on the crews' own skill in defending themselves and their planes. Knowledge of their equipment and how to use it would be a prime factor, along with any intelligence they could glean about the enemy and its attack procedure. As it was, we destroyed the German war machine, but only at the cost of countless thousands of "my boys."

At the Las Vegas Army Air Field, far from the scenes of battle, the lives of these young men depended on how well we did our job to prepare them for their missions in the B-17s—at that time the best aircraft in the war. So I was a tough instructor, not allowing any leeway. But I believe my boys understood the reasons why. At least they never complained—to me. I spent many hours working to devise teaching and training aids and procedures to improve our skills as instructors so that we might do a better job.

When the new B-29 bomber came on the scene, eventually to carry The Bomb that ended the war with Japan and opened the atomic age, we had to revamp our whole training approach because it had an electronic control system unlike the hydraulic system in the B-17.

God knows that I gave my task every ounce of earthly ability I had, and then called on him to supply the rest. He definitely helped me to engender faith and confidence in the spirits of those young men—in themselves individually, in each other, in their equipment, and in what this war was all about. I am gratified by the commendation I received as the highest rated Air Force instructor in the West Coast Training Command.

As I reflect on all of that now, though, I realize that I learned far more than I taught. Perhaps the most important lesson for me was this: When our outer shell is stripped away and we are as God would have us be, without unreal and unnecessary pride and protection, we all are brothers and sisters before God. Born and raised a Southerner, I found myself for the first time in an atmosphere without boundaries of color, sex, ethnic origin, or religion. Learning to work with all races, and to understand diverse backgrounds, was valuable beyond measure. It established in me a fundamental view of humanity that would find expression eventually in the basic concepts by which I administered Holiday Inns.

It is one of the unusual but marvelous fringe benefits of serving in the military forces, especially in time of war, to develop a profound love for one's comrades in arms. God's Word teaches that no greater love does a man have for his brother than to lay down his life for him. Only God knows how many times that happened literally in World War II—and in the wars before and since.

I can't help but wonder why those attitudes we had toward each other under those emergency circumstances cannot carry over into civilian life and our everyday relationships—the deep caring and respect we felt for the other person regardless of his differences from us. After all, everyone wants to love and be loved by their fellows. Every nationality and level of people care about their parents, family, and friends in the same way. They react to their children with the same warm concern for their happiness. They are motivated by much the same influences. They respond pretty much the same way to love. Isn't that the real significance of our equality before God?

A very special assignment came my way at Las Vegas, in addition to the B-17 training program. Colonel Henry, commanding officer of the LVAAF, must have heard of my communication record, because he called me to his office shortly after I arrived. He assigned the orientation program to me. That meant that on a Saturday morning, every fifth week or so, I would meet about one thousand arriving trainees in the post theater for their introduction to the field, and to describe what our work with them would be.

"Walton," Colonel Henry explained to me, "you must get their receiving system turned on before we can teach them anything."

That bit of wisdom underscored for me the all-important factor of motivation. With the right kind of impetus, men and women can be stirred to accomplish unbelievable tasks, to tackle challenges with a vigor that surprises even themselves. First, of course, they have to believe in themselves, then in their buddies, and then in the rightness of their mission. I was convinced this kind of confidence could be built only from the inside out, not from the outside in. This internal will to achieve excellence, to realize their dream, must be kindled by the faith that God is with them. Almost from my first day in the service, fellow

GIs would single me out as a lawyer—and one they mistakenly thought was much older than themselves—to listen to their problems and frustrations. They were frightened but didn't want anyone to know it.

"Sarge," they would say to me, "aren't you scared?"

"Sure," I would answer. "But remember, God is with you everywhere you go, always." Mama had inscribed that truth indelibly on my mind.

Looking back today, I regret that my understanding of God's Word was not deeper. I wish I had been able then to make sure they really understood God's loving promise of salvation through Jesus' death on the cross and his resurrection.

But even then, working side by side with my fellow instructors in Las Vegas—all of them mature and competent and dedicated men—I was fitting into that plan of God for my life without even being aware of it. He was using the United States government and a world war to instill in me a perception of reality and a view of human potential that in later years would be the bedrock on which I would see the world's greatest lodging system rise. The recognition of the dignity of all mankind, and the Christian principle of love for one's fellow humans, buttressed the integrity of the system at Holiday Inns.

Finally came the end to that dreadful conflict we catalog as World War II, placing it on the shelf of history and largely forgetting the millions of human lives it cost. Sadder still, we forget the lessons of that horrible experience as we callously prepare for a possible World War III.

In December 1945, together with my fellow instructors Jake, Gale, Aaron, and Shorty, we packed and stored the equipment, literally put the lock on the gate of the Las Vegas Army Air Field, and started home for Christmas via Maxwell Air Force Base, where we separated—from the service and from each other.

On January 28, 1946, I formally received my honorable discharge and joined the millions of other GIs in trying to pick up our careers and start over again in civilian ranks. For me, it was back to Memphis to resume climbing my mountain.

Now, though, I had a life partner beside me!

7 ★ The Honeymoon Garage

In late January 1946, along with my $196 in mustering-out pay from the Air Force, I brought back with me from Colorado to Memphis a wife. While I had been learning some fundamental lessons at the Las Vegas base about love for one's fellowmen in general, I also discovered an irresistible love for one beautiful woman in particular.

It all began on what the songwriter calls an "enchanted evening." Together with a buddy from the airfield, I decided to get away from the military routines and do something completely different for a change. He insisted that we go to a dance in town at the youth building of one of the churches, which was cosponsoring the event with the USO. High school fraternity dances were one thing, but I had never in my life gone to a dance at a church!

Like proper wallflowers, we took seats at the edge of the dance floor, up front near the bandstand. For awhile we just sat there listening to the music and enjoying the dancers.

A group of girls entered the room, at the end opposite the bandstand. They were members of a dancing class, I found out later, who were just in the process of learning the rhumba. The flood of light fell on a little blonde and silhouetted her in the doorway. I gasped.

"What's the matter, Bill?" my buddy asked.

Before I could answer him, I was on my feet and headed across the room. I aimed straight for the person I identified to be the chaperone. Whatever I said to her in my dazed state must have been acceptable. She took me by the hand, and introduced me to the mate God had predestined for me.

Yes. I knew that was who she was the moment I saw her across that crowded dance floor nearly two thousand miles from my home, in a place I had never intended to be, even though I didn't know at the time that she was engaged to someone else. And I have never doubted or regretted that divine appointment in the forty-plus years since.

We were determined not to be married in Las Vegas, for a number of reasons. There was another instance, as I look back on it now, where God was planting deep inside me something that would radically alter the course of my life decades later.

I had begun to develop a strong dislike for what I saw going on in the gambling houses of Las Vegas, what was then just a sleepy little Nevada town near the air base. I saw people at the gaming tables, including plenty of servicemen, who had, judging from their appearance, no business throwing away their money—their very wages. Outside the casinos were parking lots full of cars and boats people had forfeited to cover their losses. I saw them sign away deeds to real estate, probably their homes in many cases, to cover gambling debts. We heard regular reports of suicides in the hotels around that area. It was a sorry situation.

So we picked for our wedding spot the oasis in the desert which the government had built up around Boulder Dam. On October 21, 1944, the blonde this gentleman definitely preferred, Geneva Louise Chase of Denver, Colorado, and I were married by the Rev. Winston Trever in the Grace Community Church,

Boulder City, Nevada, where nobody knew us. The minister had interviewed us in the preceding weeks, and I remember him asking both of us if we were believing Christians. We promptly said yes, though neither of us had ever been instructed about the need to be born again by God's Spirit.

So, at that little church, in a Christian wedding ceremony witnessed mostly by my Air Force buddies, the foundation was laid for a lifelong love affair and partnership. We had the generous help of the ladies in the church, who brought from their homes their very best china and silver for the reception, and treated us as if we were "family." My bride, wearing her white satin wedding dress and carrying her bouquet, was surely the most beautiful girl in the world.

We had the blessing of her parents and mine, but for me there was a major disappointment. We had been in touch with my father, at that time working in San Francisco, and he had agreed to come to the wedding. Perhaps you can imagine my desperate hope that this would bring him and my mother back in touch with each other after twelve years of separation, and even help them make a new start together, to build the "family" I'd missed so much.

It wasn't to be. Before the time came, his construction company had shipped him out to the Aleutian Islands to build airstrips and housing for Air Force personnel. Just after we were married, a telegram brought word that he had dropped dead from a cerebral hemorrhage in the construction workers' hut one night while visiting with his friends, whispering his last words even as he fell: "Sweet Jesus!"

Geneva and I set up housekeeping with a few pieces of furniture in a small rented house in Henderson, Nevada, just outside Las Vegas, where she was a bookkeeper at the hospital. At our first Christmas Eve together, we got a scrawny little pine tree and made our own decorations out of popcorn and paper rings.

About ten that evening there was a knock on the door. A smiling neighbor couple stood there, offering us some of their leftover tree lights and ornaments if we could use them. Could we! And it gave us another lesson in translating "love your neighbor" into action.

Who knows what will come from a marriage, what a cornerstone for life is laid, when God—I say it reverently—is Best Man at the wedding? In the decades since, "Pug" and I have walked down life's road together, raising four wonderful children, traveling throughout the world on business trips, sharing the excitement and challenges of developing the largest hotel system in history, and struggling side by side up my mountain toward that alluring peak of *success*.

But when I first brought Geneva back to Memphis, we temporarily moved into a bedroom suite in the house where my mother lived. Very shortly, though, we prepared to set up housekeeping in one half of the garage. The slightly decrepit little building behind my mother's house on Belvedere seemed to our romance-glazed eyes like the perfect honeymoon cottage. Well, not perfect maybe, but with potential.

The remodeling project called for every skill I had ever practiced with the hammer and saw back in my old clubhouse building days. Hauling green oak two-by-fours from a lumber mill in Arkansas, tearing out space in a wall to install a bay window, putting up room partitions, planning our decorating scheme—all had the vigorous participation of Pug, who had once cherished dreams of becoming an architect. With her inspiration and my perspiration, we managed to turn the garage into a very respectable house, with one bedroom, a living room, and a kitchenette. Then began the struggles of turning that house into our home, anticipating the joys of our wonderful future together by starting our family immediately. William was born on May 25, 1947, and Geneva became a full-time mother, and helpmate to me, from that time on.

Naturally, we couldn't do all this on the $196 from the Air Force! Getting a job was a crucial priority. Geneva went to an employment agency, who got her a bookkeeping position at Gordon Transport (Jack

Gordon had been a close friend of mine in high school).

With my still-untested law degree in hand, I set out to find employment suited to my talents. I remembered that Uncle Larry Creson, of Evans, Evans, and Creson, had sort of promised me a place in his legal firm. I headed there first. Uncle Larry was sympathetic, but professional pressures forced him to favor others of the countless young lawyers returning from military service—men who had Harvard and Vanderbilt degrees, probably.

"Take advantage of the GI Bill," he advised me, "and go back for a law degree from some fine school."

After more pavement pounding, I eventually wound up appealing again for help from my old high school friend, Palmer Miller, who had gotten me into the TKO fraternity some ten years before. And again, he came to my rescue. After consulting with his partners, Palmer invited me to hang out my shingle with his firm— Johnson, Miller, and Hardison.

That proverbial lawyer's shingle took up almost all the space allotted to me—a desk in the foyer by the front door, where I sat with my back to the entrance. But I was situated, at least, and looked forward eagerly to launching my legal career with this well-respected firm.

8 ☆ Night School Lawyer at Work

We had a fairly prominent clientele—insurance
companies like the Aetna Casualty Company, local businesses like the Memphis Street Railway Company and
Union Planters Bank, and some fine old Memphis
families and their estates.

My own first cases, however, didn't exactly make the
headlines. Palmer Miller was retained by the Memphis
Street Railway Company to represent their motormen
in City Court on traffic violations. He turned these
clients over to me. At 9:30 A.M. and 2:00 P.M. each day I
was to be in attendance at court, just in case. I never
knew how many motormen might be there facing
charges until we found each other in the courtroom. I
would identify them by their gray uniforms and little
black satchels, find out the charges, and then huddle
with them to map the best defense. When there were
several at once, it could become a little hectic. But we
all survived.

The Walton family budget almost didn't survive,
though. The fee for these cases was $2.50 each, with
half to the law firm and half to me. That $1.25 per case
made me a "professional," to be sure, but hardly a
front-rank barrister!

Fortunately, I didn't have to stay at that level. The firm represented some major insurance companies, and I was given a lot of trial work—including the overload of accident investigations involving our taxi and truck clients—that sometimes got me out of bed at two in the morning. I enjoyed the trial side of things, but preparing briefs and the like left something to be desired, in my estimation. For variety, there were legal services to some excellent Memphis business clients, and general practice for the public.

One opportunity that came my way was to service, as one of my own accounts, the legal work for Bill Clark, partner in Clark and Fay, who developed residential subdivisions and eventually built the tallest office building in Memphis. I would have been the last person in the world to guess where that would lead in a few years.

I also wound up doing a lot of domestic relations cases, since senior partners in a law firm don't care for that kind of work. It wasn't a favorite of mine, either, but it contributed importantly to my reputation.

One morning in the circuit court, Judge Harry Adams said he would like to say a word about "this young lawyer," meaning me. "I don't believe there is another young lawyer practicing before this Memphis bar who has been in my court more times to dismiss divorce proceedings. In fact, I don't know if he has ever taken one to trial. Apparently, he spends an awful lot of time getting his clients reconciled, and I'd like to recommend to you other lawyers that you take a few notes on that skill. I want to commend Mr. Walton for his successful efforts in keeping couples and families together."

It is surely true that the Lord works in mysterious ways. To think that a judge would commend me for that (in just one case did I have to file proceedings because the domestic conditions were impossible) when I myself came from a broken home! And as a husband and father I put the highest priority on family unity. There is no way in this wide world that we can predict or decipher the ways of a loving Providence in equipping us to do his will. While it was true that I took pains to help my clients iron out their differences, they were primarily "cases" to me, and I was just doing my legal duty as I saw it. But there, even in my law practice, *family* was a major factor.

It was much more pleasant, I found, to help people draw up wills and plan their estates, and I had the chance to work with one that involved some of the most extensive real estate in the history of Memphis.

Then a flip of a coin changed the whole picture. The firm's senior partner, Rudolph Johnson, decided that Dallas, Texas, offered greater opportunities for his future. The remaining partners, Palmer Miller and Lee Hardison, concluded after considerable negotiation that they would go their separate ways, too. But who would keep the original office? And, more important for me, which of us young staff lawyers would go with whom? Palmer, of course, was one of my oldest friends and had helped me out on two of the most crucial occasions of my life.

Well, the partners decided the office possession question with a flip of the coin. Palmer kept the office, and Lee prepared to move out.

The other issue got a bit more complicated. A high-school friend of mine, Charles Collins, had gone to New York University following his discharge from the service, gotten his master's degree in corporate and federal tax law, and returned to Memphis. He shared my lobby area at the firm, and we had talked about practicing law together.

When the firm dissolved, Palmer offered to keep Charles and me on as associate lawyers. I deeply appreciated then, and still do, all he had done for me through the years. But Lee offered to form a new partnership with Charles and me. We couldn't resist the prospect of establishing our own firm: Hardison, Walton, and Collins.

It had the kind of ring to it that gives folks confidence. At least, we three felt pretty confident about it. The one problem we faced, though, was that at the end of the 1940s, Memphis just didn't have a square foot of office space available, even for rental.

We looked in vain for months for something suitable. Then, one day at lunch, I told my partners that I was not going back to our temporary office until I found us the right kind of space. I had an idea.

In the part of downtown Memphis where the Shelby County courthouse, city office building, and law library were located, there were some fleabag hotels, actual flophouses. One of these was one block east of the courthouse at 214 East Washington. I explored its dingy nooks and crannies and discovered that it was in very decent shape structurally.

To someone of my experience who had made pop-stands out of rusty and dented Coca Cola signs a good fifteen years before, and more recently converted a garage into a house for my bride and me, this building appeared to have definite possibilities. I searched out the owner and got an option to purchase. Somewhat surprisingly perhaps, my partners agreed. We bought the building and obtained a construction loan.

A clubhouse again! A place for my friends and me to hang out. If ever a life moved in cycles, it seemed mine did. I got out my old and trusted tools and prepared to get to work. Only this time I had to enlist some first-class help.

I turned first to my brother Van. He was destined, in later years, to become one of the most distinguished home builders in the entire mid-South, creating for his clients houses that were practically legendary in their exciting design and excellent craftsmanship. As his career prospered, he would seldom promise delivery on a new house in less than eighteen months, so meticulous was the quality he insisted on.

That spirit was already in him as we began to work together, preparing the old flophouse for its transformation. I also hired J. G. Nylin, a semiretired construction superintendent who was very good at his work, to supervise the project. Geneva actually drew up the original sketch for the building revision that we turned over to the architect. The investment company giving us the loan pointed out that we had a second floor we didn't need to use, so I went to a friend who was an accountant and leased him that upper story space before we even had ownership.

I spent as much time as possible on the job myself, not supervising, but laboring manually right beside the other workers. I used the familiar construction tools that had become like old friends to me from those earlier years right up to the time we transformed my mother's garage into our honeymoon home.

It was while I was up to my armpits in grime and sweat one day that a shadow fell across my work area. I glanced up to see a total stranger.

"What do you think you're doing?" he asked sharply.

"I'm renovating this flophouse into a law office," I replied.

"The only way to renovate anything is with a bull-dozer," he snorted.

I was to hear those words from that passing sidewalk superintendent many times over in later years, because my visitor was none other than an erstwhile movie theater operator turned housebuilder, Kemmons Wilson. But the name meant nothing to me then, and mine meant nothing to him.

I didn't like his attitude, and I guess I probably told him in no uncertain terms that it was none of his business, and suggested he leave the premises. It was then I found out that he was associated with the man who had signed a lease to rent the second story of our building as soon as it was finished. But our acquaintance went no further on that particular afternoon, and years were to pass before God's sense of humor would see fit to bring us together again—in the Home Builders Association, of all things, before the Holiday Inns venture had begun.

The work on the building went along rapidly, and we were able to take possession in October 1950. Hardison, Walton, and Collins was proud of its attractive new home, neighbor to the courthouse and the bar association library. We were the first law firm to build its own office facilities, and many others would follow our lead.

Incidentally, that office at 214 Washington Avenue was only two doors away from the old Coca Cola plant. In view of all our old associations, it seemed right that I eventually did some legal business for that company and served as lawyer for some of the routemen who had been so helpful to me when I was growing up.

We were even doing well enough financially that we could afford to help some needy people who could hardly be classified as "big fee" clients.

Now and then something mildly dramatic came along. As chairman of the zoning committee of the White Station Improvement Club, I was at the eye of the hurricane in a hard-fought zoning case representing property owners in a fine new residential area of East Memphis. The Memphis Stone and Gravel Company sought permission for gravel-washing activities that would have defaced that entire area with unsightly gravel pits and equipment. We were dealing with a stubborn petitioner, and I had to take the case through appeals all the way to the Tennessee Supreme Court before he was finally defeated—and all without any fee for me, although a lot of assistant attorneys made a handsome living off the case.

Today that area is one of the city's finest business and residential areas. I know. My younger son lives there with his wife and son.

"Good citizens should take an interest in public affairs" was a slogan I used to promote in an old-fashioned town meeting at White Station. That conviction stuck with me and motivated a lot of my activity through the years until at last it carried me right to the offices of some of the most powerful men in Washington, D.C., including the foremost occupant of the White House.

Another intricate case that I carried into the federal courts concerned a widow whose husband and son were killed in an explosion. It had involved a piece of pipe that had been purchased from a junkyard, which, in turn, had bought it from the company disassembling the munitions plant I had worked for prior to entering military service. Some big companies were arrayed against my client, and the technicalities of the accident itself were extremely complicated, but eventually I was able to secure her a generous settlement.

On the whole, though, those law years were fairly uneventful. I have to admit, too, that I never felt totally dedicated to my practice, even though I worked hard at it, put in long hours, and did the right things. After all, I had some climbing to do up that career mountain I'd selected, so I kept one eye on the business world around me, watching for a chance to break through. Offers of partnerships in major law firms came my way, but I preferred my independence in my own firm. Maybe I had an intuition that something bigger was around the next corner.

That era of my life, however, was not without some very significant developments that had nothing directly to do with the law practice. As an ambitious young attorney, I knew the value of strategic civic contacts. I was becoming the very stereotype of a "solid citizen." So I made some new friends in Kiwanis and held various offices in our neighborhood group, the White Station Improvement Club.

Each Sunday, of course, found me in prestigious Second Presbyterian Church, ushering the good members to their pews and passing the collection plate. I became a close friend of the new senior minister, Dr. Jeb Russell, whose beneficial influence guided me more and more deeply into the life and leadership of the church. Eventually I became an elder and directed a funding campaign for a new educational unit that brought in $2 million. I was doing all the right things for establishing one's community image.

One thing those straitlaced fellow Presbyterians didn't expect, though, was an old-fashioned "tent meeting." One day on a whim, I went down the street to some vacant property the church owned and caught a vision. With the full cooperation of Jeb Russell and a few other hardy saints whose names I have long forgotten, we decided to stage a one-night "revival," especially to draw in new people, including students from Memphis State University. We put up a huge tent, covered the ground with sawdust, made rows of wooden folding chairs, built a basic wooden platform on which we placed a crude pulpit (by "high church" standards!), hauled in a piano, and advertised the meeting.

The people came, filling the place. I don't know how spiritual the motives were in all of them; probably curiosity drew as many as concern did. But Jeb was in the spirit of the occasion, or the Spirit of the occasion was in Jeb, and after we had done a lot of congregational singing of hymns that were full of the oldtime religion, he preached your basic hellfire-and-brimstone evangelistic message.

Toward the end of the service, I leaned over to Geneva and wondered out loud what would happen if the preacher gave an invitation. Just then, two young people, sitting near us with their mother, got up and went forward "down the sawdust trail."

That was all it took to start a regular procession of folks moving to the front. I saw Jeb and his assistant go into a quick conference on the platform, and then they spoke most effectively to the people who were there to make spiritual decisions.

Well, Second Church was about 125 years old at the time, and that was probably twenty-five years ago. Nothing like it had happened before then that I knew about, and not since. But it said something to me that I hope I'll never forget. There is a spiritual hunger inside of people that makes them all seekers of the Lord's blessing. Whether they are church members or not, the gospel is the Good News they are looking for.

For all I know, that tent meeting, though I staged it as a kind of special event for our church, may have been God's way of setting me in a direction that eventually led to my becoming a member of the board of the Billy

Graham Evangelistic Association and chairman of the Billy Graham Crusade in Memphis. Give me a good whiff of sawdust today, and a rousing old hymn on a tinny piano, and I would feel just as much at home as if I'd been alive in the time of D. L. Moody, or even Billy Sunday in his heyday.

Church life has deepened for me over the years, even in my passages through rebellion and bitterness, and I'm glad that God kept me connected to his people back then even if I wasn't as fully aware of the spiritual score as I should have been. I know the fellowship of the family of God in his church is as vital to personal wholeness as any other family relationship on earth.

But it's more than just that. If you know what it truly means to be a Christian, "in the world but not of it," you know that you can't confine your human service to the four walls of a church building on Sundays. Through Kiwanis, believe it or not, I got into one of the most meaningful activities of my life, which I don't for a minute consider to be isolated from my Christian responsibility to love my neighbor, as Jesus taught.

It began one evening in February 1951 when I was introduced as a new member of the local chapter. The speaker was Charles Zellner, father of a mentally retarded child and president of a small group of desperate parents of such children, the "Council of Aid." He asked Kiwanis for help for those whom he described as the "forgotten children" in our affluent society.

His own son was existing as little better than a vegetable, and the doctors had told the parents there was no hope for improvement. They recommended placement in an institution so that the parents could forget him and go on with their own lives. Educators also insisted that nothing could be taught to such children—and no provision was made for them in Memphis or in Shelby County. According to Mr. Zellner, the situation was similar nationwide.

His plea touched me. Later that evening, when I was asked which committee I wanted to be assigned to, I said, "The one that will do something about Mr. Zellner's request for help."

There was no committee like that, of course. If I wanted to take on the work, and function as a committee of one, I was told, I could make an investigation and report back at the next meeting.

The following Wednesday found me in the basement of St. Mary's Cathedral, meeting with one of the most depressed groups of people I had seen in a long time. As these parents struggled to find ways to help their mentally retarded children, my heart was stirred and touched again. One of my first thoughts was to thank God for blessing me and Geneva with intelligent, healthy children. How in the world, I wondered, could I help these despairing parents?

With my limited spiritual understanding at the time, I thought of these handicapped children as God's own children—even as mine were—and that we must guide them accordingly. The abortion debate was already foreshadowed in some public discussion, but that was beside the point regarding these mentally retarded ones growing up among us. I was not a theological scholar, but my inner feelings and my common sense told me we must do everything possible to give these children the recognition and help they deserved. But the baffling question was: How?

I'm afraid my report to the Kiwanis board didn't carry much helpful information. About all I knew for sure was that the need was there, nothing was being done to fill it, and these surely were forgotten children. This was not a main area of Kiwanis service, of course. Nevertheless, they urged me to continue investigating and to come back with a plan of action.

My plan began very simply with two main components: public recognition of the need, and an assumption that these children could be helped in some way. I enlisted the cooperation of cousin Ernest Ball, the superintendent of city schools who had gotten me my work scholarship at Memphis State. He agreed to let us use a room in one of the schools for a pilot program. In the next few months we raised enough money to hire a trained teacher who developed a limited program. Almost immediately we were all encouraged to see a difference in the small group of children gathered together as they received care that made them feel important.

One day I received an urgent call to come to the school. It was not an emergency, the caller assured me, but I should hurry over. Just as I arrived at the school, I saw the dejected parents of one of the children in our program entering the building. It took me an everlastingly long minute to get up the walk and into Lenox School.

In our project room, the teacher sat beside a blue-eyed blonde girl, about five years old, who had never spoken a word in her life. As the parents and I pressed in close and waited anxiously to find out what was wrong, the teacher put his hand on the mother and said to the little girl, "Mary, say 'Mother.'"

Silence . . . for a moment . . . then "Mo-ther," Mary said hesitantly.

The teacher put his hand on the father.

"Mary, say 'Daddy.'"

"Dad-dy."

These were the first words her parents had every heard her speak. I can't begin to describe their reaction. But I can still visualize the expression on Mary's face. She knew that she had done something tremendous.

This success case was all we needed to demonstrate that all our efforts were worthwhile. The newspapers wrote up the story, the school system gave us a much larger space, and the medical profession opened their eyes and ears to look and listen. The word spread as I gave speeches and handed out brochures on "The Forgotten Child."

My own imagination flourished with a new idea. A young political hopeful named Frank Clement was aspiring to be governor of Tennessee. I made a very brash telephone call to him.

"Mr. Clement," I proclaimed, "I believe I can tell you how to get elected."

"How?" came his predictable response.

"Tennessee is at the bottom of the list of states who recognize and are doing something about the mentally retarded children in our families. Of all the children born in this country, 2 percent are afflicted in this way. They are the forgotten children. Nothing is being done to improve their lives. You can imagine the heartbreak of their parents and grandparents. Simple arithmetic will tell you how many voting age people that would add up to."

I was the lawyer now, in the courtroom, warming to the task of making my case.

"Sir," I plunged on, "you can imagine how those people would feel toward a man wanting to run for public office if he would commit himself to doing something about their children's plight. Only, of course, after investigating the situation, getting the facts, and really believing in their cause."

Apparently he was still listening, because I hadn't heard the phone click off.

"Mr. Clement," I concluded, "if you will come to Memphis, I will gladly introduce you to our program and make available to you all the facts to support what I am telling you."

When he came to Lenox School shortly thereafter, he was obviously impressed, and he was touched with all the love he saw these children give out. Back in Nashville he continued his own probing into the matter. Then, some weeks later, he went on television to announce his candidacy for governor and to outline his platform.

He was an accomplished orator, and I'll never forget his speech that evening. It seemed to me one of the most forceful I'd ever heard a politician make. Its highlight was this dramatic statement: "Fellow Tennesseans, our leaders heretofore have been guilty of nothing short of criminal negligence toward the mentally retarded children of our state. I pledge myself, if elected, to do something about it."

One of the first things Frank Clement did after he was elected governor was to institute a mental health program in Tennessee to begin to remedy the deplorable situation in our state. We started to move up on that scandalous list of neglectful states, on our way to becoming a leader in the nation's concern and attention to the problem of mental retardation.

Greatly encouraged by those developments, I began to wonder how what had happened in Tennessee might be carried to all the states. An obvious idea hit me. What about Kiwanis International?

Might the national board of directors include our program in the required activities each Kiwanis Club in the United States should undertake? Would the national board be willing to investigate and take aggressive action to improve the plight of the mentally retarded children across the whole country?

Happily, their response was positive. Their investigation found the program deserving, and they did include it as a National Required Action for all Kiwanis clubs beginning in 1954—in fact, as one of the three major headings. Throughout the nation, and even the world, the "forgotten child" began to be sympathetically noticed and helped. Local and national legislation began to be formulated to provide for those unfortunate boys and girls the educational benefits available to other American children.

Meanwhile, back in Memphis, I was asked to prepare the documents to charter a national organization to formalize the support needed for programs throughout the United States. This charter of March 1953 set the pattern for the National Association for Retarded Citizens and became one major influence in focusing public attention on mental health.

My job was done. I had a warm feeling of personal satisfaction as I made my final committee report to the local Kiwanis chapter. The project had added new meaning to my own life.

In my own family situation, something remarkable had happened also while I was busy with the law practice and various civic activities. Though Geneva and I had started our Memphis life together rather inconspicuously, if not inauspiciously, in the remodeled garage behind my mother's Belvedere Avenue house, a truly major move occurred in 1947. We purchased three homes on Pelham Circle, in a new development in East Memphis called "Pleasant Acres." One was for Kackie and Mama, my mother and grandmother, one was for sister Betty and her husband, and the third was for Geneva and me—and our intended increase in the family! In fact, my mother's sister, Aunt Celeste Creson, fell in love with the area, too, so she and her husband got a house near the rest of us.

I contracted for the three new houses and put the Belvedere house in the hands of a realtor friend. It didn't sell. Lots of people have known the same feeling of panic that increasingly gripped our three households as the closing date drew near on the Pelham Circle properties—but I stayed calm, confident things would work out. I relieved the realtor of his obligation and assumed personal responsibility to sell the old house. This didn't particularly reassure the rest of my folks, and it made them more than a little impatient with me. One morning at breakfast I was interrupted by a knock on the door. A man had seen the For Sale sign in the front yard and had just stopped by to inquire. Well, as any tenacious salesman will say, "I didn't turn him loose" until I had signed him up to buy our place for about $20,000—enough for the down payments on the new properties. The Lord had come through again in answer to prayer, confirming his presence with us! And, as usual, the way the Waltons were housed had motivated my move. We arrived at Pleasant Acres on Labor Day 1947. Our new lots exceeded an acre each, and I spent many happy hours working in the yard. The houses were bought in what was called "semifinished" condition, so every night after I got home from work there was plenty of interior painting and trim installation and the like to do. And with our flair for design and construction, Geneva and I seemed always to be making additions to the house, as well as to the family.

With my mother and grandmother next door, and sister across the street, we adults enjoyed each other's company. I was a struggling young lawyer; Betty's husband was trying to start up his medical practice; brother Van did his stint in the Korean War and then came home to begin his efforts in the home construction business. None of us had any money, but we had an extended family happiness together that couldn't be beat. We would have Saturday night suppers together out in the backyard, at Christmas we would decorate the whole neighborhood, and at Easter there would be egg hunts for the all the children to enjoy when they came home from church and Sunday school, all dressed up in their fancy outfits.

In this kind of compound our children were born and grew up together—with our grandmother and mother, we brothers and sister and brother-in-law, our aunt, and what eventually accumulated to be nine cousins— living in a storybook setting for the next sixteen years.

Betty's husband, Dr. James L. Alston, went on to become a renowned physician and a pioneer in surgical procedures; my brother Van became noted as one of the finest home builders in this whole part of the country; and I would soon play my role in developing the largest hotel system in the industry. We were following different paths and we were getting prosperous by every material standard. But we knew the meaning of family togetherness, of sharing our love, that no amount of money could buy. And we knew the bond of sharing sorrow, too. There my grandmother, and much later my mother, died.

I'm tempted sometimes to ask myself: "What if I had stayed on Pelham Circle? What if . . . ? What might have been?" The next Walton move after about sixteen years was destined to change a lot of things because it reinforced my supreme desire to climb higher up that mountain of success that I found more and more alluring.

A man can't help but wonder what might have been waiting down the road he turned away from in favor of another. But that is not given us to know, in the Lord's wisdom, or we might never finish the course we are on.

At last, something happened on which my whole career future hinged, though I could not know that at the time. Bill Clark invited me to lunch one day and suggested I should consider getting out of law practice and into the business world, because he thought he saw in me the signs of a good administrator. He wanted me to meet a man named Kemmons Wilson, who would be president of the Home Builders Association for the next year, and to talk with him about a position there.

When I got home to Pelham Circle that night, I cried on Geneva's shoulder. Literally. We sat beside each other on the back steps after the children were in bed, and I wept bitter tears. My efforts to improve my partnership standing at the law firm had proved futile, and now along comes a mere desk job possibility—with home builders of all things!

In the midst of my moaning, Geneva suddenly electrified me by saying, "Bill, God has a plan for your life, and you've just got to have faith in him to work things out."

Here was my wife repeating exactly what my grandmother had always told me. With God using women to gang up on me that way, what else could I do but keep on hoping for the best, even in the face of what looked mediocre?

When the meeting with Kemmons came about, he told me he had two goals for his term in office—an office building for the Association, and a home show the likes of which Memphis had never seen before. Thus I was officially introduced to the entrepreneur who would keep me on the jump for the next twenty years—the same man I'd told to mind his own business when he had stopped by my office renovation site years before!

A small group of about a half dozen men, who represented the power brokers in the business community, all
coming from the old-line blueblood families that literally ran our city, were the board members of the
Home Builders Association. They treated me to dinner
at the swankiest club in town to court me, I guess, for
the position Bill Clark had told me about. Kemmons
was there, of course, as president. At that meeting, by
the way, for the first time in my life that I could remember, I laid eyes on a man named Wallace Johnson.

With my law practice well regarded, and my civic
activities giving me some minor public prominence, my
dinner hosts formally invited me that night in 1954 to
become the legal counsel and acting administrative officer of the Home Builders Association of Memphis. I
was flattered, of course, that the ranking Memphian
aristocrats even knew I existed, much less wanted me
to work for them.

Now, doesn't that job offer, despite my misgivings,
seem like a natural kind of connection for this Walton
boy who had been preoccupied with housing concerns
from early childhood? Pop-stands to clubhouses to B-17
and B-29 mock-ups to garage conversion to flophouse
renovation into a law office—the construction industry
surely was not anything new to me.

Frankly though, at the time, I didn't see any particular
reason to get excited about the prospect at all—except
that the title executive vice president they held out as
bait suggested that maybe I was getting a firmer footing
on that mountain climb to success than I ever had before. I accepted their proposition, not only on its own
merits (which were a bit dubious), but partly out of
frustration with the practice of law where, though
successful, I didn't have any deep feeling of fulfillment
or solid prospect of advancement. Some part of my
personality was not contented with legal routines
anymore.

Their chief concern at that meeting was who would
construct the new building. Not one of the board of
building experts was willing to do it, because they

knew the rest would constantly be looking over their shoulder and meddling! So, Kemmons declared, "Let Bill do it."

"Nothing doing," I said. "I've got a law practice to wind up, and I don't want a bunch of home builders telling me how to erect a commercial building—which I don't know how to do in the first place."

"I'll oversee the project," Kemmons said, "and anybody who wants to butt in will have to come to me and leave you alone."

As it worked out, they left me completely alone—so completely that I couldn't get any construction advice from anybody even when I asked for it. For that very reason, I almost lost my life on that construction job.

The roof of the Home Builders Association office building was being tar-coated, and I went up on it about five one morning to check things out. I had volunteered to start the fires under the tar pots in order to save some money. I had just finished stoking the fire with lumber under a fifty-five-gallon drum of tar and was walking away from it when it exploded and ignited, sending boiling hot tar flying all over that roof area and narrowly failing to burn me alive. Nobody had bothered to tell me you had to make an opening in the top of the drum or lift the lid slightly when it was being heated up. The fire department capably handled the emergency, but it took a couple of days to clean up the roof mess, and longer than that to get all the tar off the new brick wall.

I built them their building within $300 of my $16,000 budget, with the cooperation of vendors and subcontractors they did business with. That tiny overrun was all Kemmons could see, and he gave me royal heck for it. It made me wonder if this new boss of mine had an appreciative bone in his whole body. The question would become commonplace in succeeding years.

Another one of my major responsibilities in the new position was to put together the Memphis Home Show Kemmons wanted, with help from—who else?—the

Coca Cola Company. As the writer of Ecclesiastes says, "There is nothing new under the sun." I mustered my little flair for showmanship, that hadn't had much chance to flourish in the law practice, and we got up a wing-ding of a show that probably set the stage, literally, for what would follow in the Holiday Inns years.

The Lord obviously had better things in store for me than to let my life end in a tar bath when I was thirty-four years old. After all, there was that plan that Mama had always kept talking to me about.

When I was a child I had always taken my grandmother's assurances at face value because I believed so implicitly in her. But as life moved on, the very notion of such a plan tended to get lost in the shuffle of career-building, community service, and family life.

When the move into the Home Builders Association came, I didn't really perceive it to be the threshhold of the "Great Disclosure." But, even though I couldn't see it, all the main pieces of the plan were now in place.

First of all, early misfortunes in our family, climaxing with my father's leaving, had stimulated an entrepreneurial spirit in me. I grew up facing challenges. I had no choice but to use my wits and skills to meet them. My guiding motto could have been "Nothing ventured, nothing gained." It turned out, of course, in my coming years at Holiday Inns, that risk-taking would be practically my way of life.

Then, also, in struggling so painfully for peer acceptance during public school years, I discovered the secret of human respect—valuing people for their personal virtues. My position on the social scale, and my lack of certain advantages, were not used against me as bars to friendship, except by a few misguided snobs. Other young people willingly took interest in me for my own sake, not because of my credentials or connections. This ingrained in me an appreciation for people as people that laid the moral foundation for my later career.

One other piece of God's very logical plan, unfolding for me as a young adult, generated in me a passion for motivating people to produce to their highest capacity. In my DuPont job, and then in Air Force service, I became increasingly sure that *attitude* meant everything in determining *action.* That conviction would be the cornerstone of my management philosophy at Holiday Inns.

But all this time Holiday Inns didn't even exist. The Lord, with his infallible sense of perfect timing, was getting me ready for something that wasn't there. To prove that he always knows what he is doing, he had fitted in the key piece of the plan—which, to me, still looked more like a puzzle. Through the law practice which led to the Home Builders assignment, he had put me in exactly the right position to be found by a couple of visionary businessmen at exactly the time when they needed a Bill Walton.

Mama was right. I can see that now, looking back over my life. But she saw it looking ahead. She knew that was the meaning of faith. I still had a lot to learn about that. But when the next moment came to make a move, I practically leaped—right out into thin air.

Thus far, between the ages of twelve and thirty-two, I had been an organizer of systems in industry, a trainer of teams in the military, a small business operator in college, a private builder on an exceedingly modest scale, an instigator of community social reform, and an attorney for the last half of those two decades.

We never know, do we, when we dump the pieces of a jigsaw puzzle out of a box onto the tabletop, how the pieces are going to fit together to form a sensible design. Yet, Mama doggedly insisted the puzzle was a plan. She never doubted God's capacity to create order out of chaos in one person's life, since he had been able to do it on the cosmic scale of the universe, according to her well-read Bible. I put a lot of confidence in Mama, but her God was not as real to me personally as he was to become later. I believed he existed, and I talked to him about my need for wisdom and courage, and I tried as best I knew how to be a decent man both personally and professionally. But there was a whole lot about him that I had never even guessed as I reached my mid-thirties.

I had yet to learn, for instance, that he has a terrific sense of humor.

9 ★ Picnic and Panic

In 1954 the Almighty Creator of the universe and the
Father of mankind, Mama's God, concentrated his su-
pernatural sovereignty on Memphis, Tennessee, and
arranged for the plan that was to occupy Bill Walton
for the next thirty years and beyond to fall into place at
a picnic.

It was a custom of the Home Builders Association to
hold an annual outing, and that year they had picked
the Italian Country Club—and I do mean "country," so
far out of town that I didn't even know such a place
existed. In that relaxed setting, the characteristically
tough and gruff builders proved themselves capable of
enjoying a lot of fun together, playing baseball and
other games, or just sitting around under the shade
trees swapping stories and having good conversation.

Kemmons and Wallace were enjoying their cool bottles of Orange Crush off to the side of the ball field
where I was playing in the game. Kemmons, by the
way, held the Orange Crush distributorship, so I suppose he might have been the supplier for that picnic. I
think it was Wallace who called me over.

"Bill, my partner has an idea, a good one, that we've
been trying to get off the ground for the past couple of

years. The time has come when we need a man who can dedicate his full effort to that project, because we're both too busy with our home building and other enterprises."

"It's an idea," Kemmons broke in, "that's bound to make somebody a lot of money. We'd like to know if you'd be interested in taking it over, even though it would mean leaving your law practice completely."

Well, they had my attention.

"I'll help you," he added quickly. I laughed, and reminded him of the way he had promised to help me with the Association job, and how leaving me literally helpless had almost gotten me killed up on the roof.

I think it was Wallace who said, "We don't have a lot of money. But we'll each put up $250 a month, and that will give you enough for bacon and eggs for your family."

I commented to them that I had reached the end of the starvation period for a young lawyer, that my partners and I owned our own office building, and that things were going along pretty well for me.

Kemmons pressed the case by commenting that this project would bring me more money than I had ever heard of in the law practice. "This can be just as big as you want to dream and want to make it," he said.

I thought hard while they talked for the next ten or fifteen minutes. Then I said, "OK, let's go."

Kemmons said they would call me in a few days. Sure enough, shortly later he invited me to come over to his home one evening. It was late fall, 1955.

As we sat down in a little den off the front entrance of his house, he began by talking about his reputation around town as a wheeler-dealer. The fact was, he and a partner operated a pinball machine business that some folks in the civic leagues had gotten after him about, suspecting that the players' payoffs might be in something other than just candy or prizes. The houses he built were generally in the low-cost bracket, and some owners had made complaints after moving in. We didn't go into details about his local public relations problems, however, and he moved on quickly to the heart of the matter.

"You're going to run this operation, Bill," he said, "any way you want to, any way you're big enough to do it. I know it's going to make a lot of money."

He then began to outline what I'd have to do: organize a corporation so that we could franchise the right to build motels, which he was calling "Holiday Inns," a name he told me I would have to get a patent for. He said I was free to hire and build my own management team because the only other people involved at that time were Elmer C. "Jack" Ladd and Ernest B. "Barney" McCool.

He characterized Jack as the best salesman he had ever seen, and Barney was brother to Wallace Johnson's wife, Alma. Already they had tried with little success to sell a few franchises to some of their fellow home builders at the annual NAHB convention in Chicago. Then they came up with plan B: invite seventy-five active and progressive home builders they knew to come to Memphis and hear about the new venture. This time they got several to sign up, but only a half dozen or so actually got busy and started motel construction after they went home.

"Here's where you come in," he said to me. "We want to take this company public so that we can generate more activity among the franchisees. The big benefit to you is that we'll give you some stock options."

At that point in my life, I really didn't understand the value of stock options. Nevertheless, the whole idea attracted my venturesome nature. My vision and imagination began to picture Holiday Inns covering the whole nation and spreading around the world. Maybe unconsciously the old pride in my ancestor innkeeper of two centuries earlier, Captain Walton, stirred anew.

"Up to now, Bill," Kemmons said, "I've never gone into a venture where, if it failed, anybody would get hurt except me. I've never been willing to risk the career of another man."

Those words would haunt me much later.

"Have we got a deal?" he asked.

"Yep, we've got a deal."

We shook hands.

"As of now," he said, "you are officially 'Holiday Inns.' "

October 1955. It began.

After further talk about my winding up my law business matters and getting into the preliminaries of organizing Holiday Inns, I left. As I drove home to Pelham Circle, I said to myself: "Bill Walton, you have just lost your mind. You know you can't support your family and do other necessary things on $500 a month."

As soon as I got home I went into the bedroom and sat down. I decided I had better talk to the Lord about this. "Lord, if this is something that you think I ought to do, someway let me know."

At that point in my life I was not a knowledgeable Christian, even though I was a believer. I knew that my limitations as a night school lawyer left me without the necessary sophistication for something as ambitious and technical as taking a company public. I knew nothing about franchises. I knew nothing about patent law. But I was willing to take it on, I told the Lord, "if you will help me."

Maybe my theology was askew, and I should have said, "If you will do it for me, Lord," but I was praying the best I knew how then.

In the meantime I'd been talking with my partner, Lee Hardison, and he told me he thought I was making a mistake. "Just on general principles," he said, "I'm going to leave your name as partner on the door of this office for a minimum of at least a year after you leave here. Then we'll see how this deal is going, and you will have a fallback position."

True to his word, he left the sign unchanged until sometime in 1957.

Before long, Kemmons called me to meet with his lawyer, John Martin. The scheduled meeting was held in a room in one of Kemmons' four Memphis Holiday Inns at 980 South Third Street, with just Kemmons, Wallace, Martin, and me. John was a stickler for details (his father had been a judge), and he minced no words in describing the situation.

"Kemmons and Wallace," he said, "I've told you that what you've got here is a naked franchise deal. If you keep selling that deal over the country, you're trading in interstate commerce. But you don't have all these things that you say you have in your sales presentation. If you keep doing that, you're going to wind up going to jail. You better make up your minds right now that you are going to let this young lawyer," pointing at me, "do something about putting some meat on the bones of this naked deal."

He went on to talk about the things he felt needed to be done, and done in a hurry, mostly matters concerning the organizational structure. Jack Ladd and Barney McCool were out selling a "system" that included (or claimed to include) architectural plans and specifications, finance consultation, legal advice, interior decorating, employee training, and other promises.

To add to my worries, around Christmas time, one of my friends and an old-line Memphis builder, Mr. Chandler, had called me aside to say he thought I was making a terrible mistake to walk away from the law practice and the Association to join up with Kemmons. He didn't know the half of it. Kemmons and Wallace had told me they didn't have any more capital to put into start-up operations, so I'd just have to get whatever money I needed from the sale of franchises. (I didn't even know at the time that the two partners were already in debt on the project to the tune of $37,500.)

That was the raw material I had to start with on New Year's Day 1956, when I had cleared the decks of everything else and was ready to put all my time into the urgent task awaiting me.

"Holiday Inn" was the name sketched in on the drawings the architect brought to Kemmons, and he liked the sound of it. Besides, unknown to me at the time, he was in a deal with a hotel operator out in Danbury, Connecticut, who called his place "Holiday Inn." So that became the corporation's name—some ten years after Bing Crosby had made it famous in his movie. Believe me, there was nothing as romantic about our start as the picturesque country place in New England featured in the film! We needed Bing!

10 ⋆ No! Not a Dirt Floor

We had to set up shop somewhere, and they told me Wallace had a building at 887 Rayner that could be "fixed up" for use as an office. History surely has a way of repeating itself. There I was again, having to do my own manual labor to prepare the headquarters for the new Holiday Inns company. It had been a plumbing shop whose owner had gone bankrupt, a building that was set down in the middle of a combination lumber and coal yard, with railroad tracks running nearby.

I walked into the building for the first time on a cold, rainy day in January. It had a brick facade, with corrugated metal siding and a flat roof. Part of the floor in one of the back rooms was plain dirt. The place was smelly, the venetian blinds at the windows were tattered and hanging at all angles, and I had a sick, sinking feeling about what I was getting myself into. Nobody had any money, and here we were trying to start a new nationwide business in a building that was literally junk! It was a different universe entirely from the comfortable, paneled law office I had just vacated. How in the world could we ever make this thing work?

I was plain scared as well as depressed. I really had trouble that day mustering up much vision and imagination!

So I prayed, "Lord, what have I gotten into? You'll just have to show me what to do and give me the wisdom to make the right decisions." Then I added, probably for the first time in my life, "And I'll try to do everything to please you."

Have you ever been tempted to bargain with God, to strike a deal of some kind? At this distance in time from that gloomy moment, I'm willing to admit that I might just have been trying to "con" the Lord, using him because I didn't have anybody else to turn to, not because I had such great confidence in his power and faithfulness.

I know that I don't like to be the speaker on somebody else's program simply because they couldn't find anybody else, and I daresay God isn't all that pleased that we wait to turn to him only as our last resort in trouble. People are doing that all the time in crisis moments of their lives, only to go on with business as usual when the emergency is over.

But I have to add also that I wasn't demanding that God give me proof of anything. As I understand the Bible, he wants us to trust him as a little child would. Believe me, as a thirty-five-year-old "child," I couldn't do more than trust him, as Mama had always told me to do.

Well, *mopping* was needed more than *moping!* Jack and Barney pitched in with scrub brushes and pails and helped me clean the buildings, along with a boy just out of high school, Dudley Beale.

Once we got it semiclean we painted it. We had no furniture, so I went back into one of Wallace's lumber warehouses on the property and commandeered several slab doors to lay across boxes to serve as desks, which we spray-painted black. My spirits began to rise—just a little. (Wallace later accused me of "stealing" those doors, but from what I could judge, his business wasn't exactly booming at the time and these were slightly warped castoffs to begin with.) A couple of small auxiliary rooms that we also cleaned up became the accounting department and the legal department. Kemmons let us have a mimeograph machine that Dudley knew how to run, and Wallace came up with a couple of old typewriters, so we were ready at least to send out memorandums.

That was the auspicious beginning we made in the first quarter of 1956. But already we were being threatened by possible lawsuits for not delivering on the franchise contract guarantees. Kemmons wanted me to call a meeting of all the franchisees immediately, but I knew we weren't ready to face them, so I got him to back off from that for awhile.

What was going through my mind? The same persistent question as always: "What do I do now?" I did the only thing I knew how as a lawyer—to make a good investigation. So I shut myself up with the existing sketchy franchising agreement and began to study it, line by line, making my own revisions as I felt necessary.

Inspiration suddenly struck, and I called the president of Coca Cola in Atlanta, remembering how the law library in Memphis had held several volumes of that company's cases. In those days you didn't have top business leaders isolating themselves behind fancy and intimidating titles like chief executive officer, so they were fairly easy to reach by a little guy like me. Nowadays it has become an ego trip for a lot of top managers who practically want a band to play "Hail to the Chief" whenever they come into the room.

The president was sympathetic to the point of offering to put me in touch with his own legal officer, Mr. Bayol, who handled specific matters concerned with protecting the corporate name. He gave me all kinds of sage advice, especially about staying clear of lawsuits for the first five years. He explained that the name was not a "trademark" but a "service mark," protectable under federal law if we were doing interstate commerce.

One thing he explained carefully was that the services to be identified with a service mark must be unique, almost like a patent. When I outlined for him things that we were doing that had never been done before in the lodging industry—children free, free TV in every room, swimming pool, no key deposit, baby-sitter references, doctor on call, dog kennel and pet food—he knew we were unique for sure.

A few weeks later he was in Memphis on business and made a point of spending a couple of days with me in the middle of all his other professional obligations, during which time he tutored me so thoroughly in the laws governing service marks that I think I became an expert on the subject. I shall never cease to appreciate how a big company like Coca Cola cared enough for the little fellow trying to get started that they would give that degree of attention.

He stressed a lesson I never forgot—that diligence in protecting our name was of supreme importance, overriding even some of the legal technicalities. There must be no dilution or adaptation of the name's use, right down to the size and style and color of print on our signs and other materials.

We also registered slogans: "The Nation's Innkeeper," "Fireside Human Relations," "The fine old innkeeping tradition in a modern setting," as well as the "Great Sign" with its flashing star, and some other distinctives as we developed them in future years. We were to see to it that, under no circumstances, now or in the future, would the company or any of its franchisees deviate in the slightest degree from any of those specifications that made the name Holiday Inns unique.

I remember when we built our first high-rise Holiday Inn on Lake Shore Drive in Chicago, a real hotel in the finest sense of the word, with a revolving restaurant on the rooftop that gave diners a marvelous view of the lake and the park and the city skyline. The manager we hired to be the innkeeper was of the old school. He said to me: "Surely, Mr. Walton, you don't intend for us to include a dog kennel in an establishment like this!"

But to maintain the integrity of the system, to preserve that distinctive meaning of the name Holiday Inn, we went down into the lower level parking garage and saw to it that we built a dog kennel! No deviation. As a result of this kind of insistence by management, travelers always knew what to expect when they stopped over at a Holiday Inn. No surprises. What the name said is what we delivered. But it took constant diligence to prevent dilution, just as Mr. Bayol had said.

If business isn't your calling, this all may sound like just so much ancient history and corporate technicality now. But there was, and is, a principle at stake that seems to me utterly urgent to reaffirm in times like these. Shakespeare's old question, "What's in a name?" and another expression we sometimes hear in the business world, "They're just trading on their name," point to an issue that we have to take seriously as Christians.

Are we as concerned and particular to see that there is no dilution of that "Name above every name" when we presume to apply it to ourselves? Is "Christian" just a general noun or modifier we can toss around to cover anything moral or ethical or even religious? Or does the name really *mean* something?

Sometimes people use the name as though it were a synonym for *American,* or they talk about some act of human kindness as "the Christian thing to do." I've learned enough by now to know that, in the business world at least, there are scores of men and women who call themselves Christians who have never had a life-changing introduction to Jesus Christ, even though they may be loyal and devout churchgoers. We as a company were simply one illustration of the universal principle I'm talking about. Holiday Inns went to great pains to insure that our name would stand for something in particular that the public would always recognize and could always count on.

That's what the Coca Cola people taught me. Another person who gave me invaluable help was my cousin out in San Francisco, Sam Stewart, retired vice chairman of the board of the Bank of America there. Sam had been a corporate attorney in New York City, where he authored the maritime law that governs New York harbor. We were good friends, and I felt free to call him on the phone anytime during those formative months and years. He became practically a step-by-step consultant to me.

Geneva tells me I make too much of the fact that I was only a night school lawyer, and maybe she is right that I downgrade that background. The fact is that my certification qualified me to practice law from the local and district level all the way up to the United States Supreme Court, so I did know something about the law.

I even knew more about current business administration theory and practice than I gave myself credit for, through the help of my old high school buddy, Allen Webb, who went on to the Harvard School of Business. There they used what they called the case method, and Allen would send these to me when he was through with them along with all his lecture notes and papers while I was studying law back in Memphis. So I did have some familiarity with business administration by this informal "correspondence" method.

The Lord has all kinds of ways to supply our needs, whether it is manna from heaven or water from a rock, as he did for Moses. We may have been raw beginners, but we weren't rank amateurs—and we kept on learning as we grew through the years.

Even though my early prayers were stumbling, and possibly superficial, they were sincere, and I clung to the belief that the way we were doing things was God's answer to my plea for his help.

That is what I have always trusted him for, because he is the Father and I am his child. That's what I hope will always be the true representation of my own name, both as a man and as a follower of Jesus Christ.

A name, I'm convinced, is more than an ID tag like we wear on our coat or dress at a convention. It is more than what we are called. Even if it is a common name like John or Mary Smith, shared with 10 million other John and Mary Smiths, our name is the symbol of our character, of what we believe in and what we stand for. If we are in conversation about the Smiths and any confusion arises, someone will say: "Oh, you mean *that*

John Smith." The *that* is the point. Each of us is
responsible for the meaning of our name.

When it comes to the family of God, people will
interpret the name "Christian" by the meaning we give
it in our words and actions. And because God has an
Enemy who is always trying to slander that name, we
are right back to that admonition to diligence in living
up to its true uniqueness. The Bible clearly defines
what the name means. The question is, how does our
life translate Christian for our family, friends,
neighbors, social acquaintances, and business
associates?

I had to carry the same faith into my home life. All
idealism aside for the moment, that $500 a month they
were paying me didn't stretch far, with making
mortgage payments, buying a secondhand washing
machine for Geneva, and covering our regular
household expenses. If that new company in the
converted plumbing shop went down the drain, the
whole Walton family could go right down with it. So,
while part of my motivation to strive for success was
the Wilson dream I now shared, another part was the
Walton desperation of sheer survival, for me and my
loved ones.

My biggest obstacle to getting things moving was that
franchise plan. I had been making pretty satisfactory
progress in my climb up the success mountain during
those years in the law practice, but now it was almost
as if I had tumbled back down to the base and had to
start all over again. That prospect of a fresh beginning
appears to be one thing to a newlywed, honorably
discharged serviceman, with a crisply authentic law
diploma in his hand. But the outlook is radically
changed when you walk away from the security of an
established life-style as you approach middle age.

More and more people know what I'm talking about
because of the volatility of the job market these days.
Many causes have combined—in economics, politics,
technology, and even psychology—to undermine a
person's confidence in employment security. You never

know when you are going to be replaced by a robot, or given early retirement to make way for new blood. *Tenure* and *seniority* and even *contract* are just words.

Maybe that is part of the explanation for the resurgence of the entrepreneurial spirit in our free enterprise system. People figure that if they can't count on some established company to supply a regular paycheck, they will just start a business of their own and be their own boss. These personal incorporations run into the thousands every year—and a whole lot of them fail. But some succeed.

The point is that new starts are not out of the question at any age. Here I am now, past sixty-five, getting into a whole different aspect of service to God by putting out a book like this that draws upon all that the Lord has taught me through my years of ups and downs in the business world.

A lot of men and women in retirement just sit around and vegetate, or play games with each other in what has sometimes been accurately called "second childhood," when they could be capitalizing on their decades of accumulated experience and wisdom to launch new enterprises. What would have happened to the people of Israel in their Egyptian bondage if Moses had retired from shepherding when he was sixty-five? For him, in the plan of God, the age of eighty became a starting point for the most significant work he had ever undertaken in his whole life, and he was to be granted another forty years to get the job done!

Who can tell how much life extension the Almighty will grant to someone who is obeying his commission to tackle a task that is perfectly timed for the later stages of life? You know what I think? God has never retired anybody who labors in his Kingdom. Sometimes he transfers or relocates or reassigns them here on earth, but eventually he promotes them to heaven, where the work of glorifying him never stops and where they will never get tired nor run out of delightful assignments to colabor in his eternally creative will.

I wish I'd been smart enough, or spiritual enough, to think thoughts like that back on Rayner Street as I sat at my homemade desk and looked out the dingy window at the coal yard! But there were plenty of hours, even days, when I felt far more like I was stuck in a hole than climbing a mountain. If only I had understood better then what the plan of God for a person's life means, I could have spared myself a lot of chain-smoking and nail-biting anxiety.

But there I sat, "trusting God" and trying to organize a corporation and a franchise system for which I had so little direct preparation! Or so I thought. In his infinitely ingenious way, God is always preparing us for what is next, because his wisdom comprehends the entire plan from start to finish, and he knows precisely how all the seeming jumble of our experience fits together.

Mulling over this franchise business in my little office, I could not possibly foresee that the Holiday Inns system would eventually span the globe with nearly two thousand lodging establishments.

As it was, Kemmons already was dreaming big about a chain of four or five hundred inns, reaching from coast to coast in this country, although what we had at the moment was only four very modest places in Memphis plus a handful of shaky franchises. Can you imagine what a mess the organization would have gotten into as it developed through the years if every local manager had been at liberty to run things according to his own wisdom or whim?

I suppose if I had known what lay ahead, the sheer magnitude of it would have paralyzed me. But my mandate was to formulate the charter and by-laws for a system, and that meant a plan that would coordinate highly diverse leadership and location factors into a smooth operation in which all the gears meshed properly. Deviation would strip those gears and leave the corporate machine on the junk heap.

There was yet another serious complication to my problem. The men who had bought franchises thus far

were not a bunch of country bumpkins or greenhorns.
If I had been dealing with boys fresh out of school, I
could have slapped together a plan that none of them
would dare question because they had no experience.
But the owners of these Holiday Inns were highly successful men in business, the professions, and the trades,
who had enough spare capital lying around for them to
venture some new investments. They all knew they
were taking a certain amount of risk, of course, because the idea was untested. But they were not putting
their money into this paper dream out of charitable
impulses; they were counting on a good financial
return—and they had heard Kemmons' glowing words
about "making a lot of money."

Some of those men might have been willing to hire
me as their lawyer in the past, but why should they
trust me to know what I was doing in organizing a business—which was their field of expertise and achievement? As I've said, some of them were already angry
enough to take us to court over our failure to deliver
what the contract called for.

Pressure? I felt like an ant in the path of a steam
roller. Our "legal department" was one file drawer, and
our "training program" was whatever the staffs of the
four Memphis motels happened to be doing as they
flew this operation by the seat of their pants.

I doubt that I ever actually thought this, but I
wouldn't be surprised if subconsciously I might have
wondered if even God himself understood a franchise
system, since it was all so innovative, and he had done
his creating an awful long time ago!

How could he resolve my dilemma? In my need for
some practical help, the Lord faithfully brought to my
remembrance the Air Force base in Nevada and the GI
Joes I had been responsible to train. To train for what?
To train them to function, with all their diverse apti-
tudes and attitudes, as one single entity—a bomber
crew. There was the cue I needed, right out of the
wartime emergency, and it became the core of my
franchising philosophy: *unity*. Not everybody doing

their own thing, but everybody combining their efforts in one synchronized system.

The term I used for it from then on was "Integrity of the System," because I knew the word *integrity* meant *wholeness*, and we were going to function as a *whole*— every part fitting and performing harmoniously.

So many of our human efforts lack integrity—not honesty, or sincerity, or devotion—but a certain element that fits everything together to make sense. We do things, perfectly worthy things in themselves, piecemeal. Our life activity amounts to just an accumulation of fragments. No wonder we feel frustrated that we are not getting anywhere, even when what we are doing is valuable and helpful to others! It can happen to us in Christian service and in church organizations just as readily as anywhere else, because we are constantly pressured to think in the world's ways and follow the world's patterns instead of biblical models and principles that the Holy Spirit wants to teach us.

Drawing on that military background then, I worked over the skeleton contract again and again, devising components of the system that would be unalterably required of all inn owners, and deciding which operations might be left to local discretion.

External compulsion had to be balanced with internal motivation that the goal of success was worth striving for, and that every person was indispensable in reaching it. After all, any good system that involves human beings in a common enterprise will be a harness to amplify their energies, not a straitjacket to restrict them.

I'm not just playing on words. If *integrity*—wholeness— was one foundation block for the Holiday Inns company, another had to be *individuality*—respect for each person's God-given capabilities. The addition of this concept to my thinking was a catalyst in the management philosophy that ultimately emerged.

One of my most treasured possessions is a personal letter to me from Alfred P. Sloan, Jr., longtime chairman of General Motors, written in November 1964 after I had complimented him on his excellent new book, *My Years with General Motors.* I had been so thrilled to discover that many of his guiding principles were identical to mine in the formation of Holiday Inns, Inc., and told him that I had made his book required reading for all our company officers as a study volume.

At the end of his letter, Mr. Sloan imparted a choice bit of that earthy wisdom for which he was so renowned: "Just as it is true that one suit of clothes does not fit all individuals, no plan of management will fit all enterprises. We have to get what ideas we can and make the adjustments necessary."

That reflects exactly the conviction that motivated my approach to data-gathering for the franchise agreement. Through letters and phone calls to the franchisees, I practiced what I was preaching. I solicited their ideas and perspectives, and I listened to them tell their experiences in building up their own successful businesses. It gave me a tremendous crash course in business administration, at the same time that it helped me understand how far I could go in regimenting them.

Respect for the individual. It is vital to every kind of human interaction, including business dealings, for the simple reason that God made us in his image—which is a wonder and a glory in itself—and he sovereignly gifted each of us with something precious to contribute to the wholeness of human life on earth.

I know people, and have worked with them—yes, even at Holiday Inns—whose words are socially correct but whose actions spring from a basic attitude of contempt for their fellows. Such people think the universe revolves around themselves and that everything and everyone in it is to be exploited for their own satisfaction.

In all my years of running daily operations at Holiday Inns, I can honestly say that the franchisees were my best friends in the world, mainly on account of the respect I showed for their individual dignity from the start and continued to demonstrate toward them in all the years that followed. The parent company in Memphis treated the franchisees the way any parents should treat their offspring—giving them firm guidance from the home office, and at the same time allowing them considerable authority to formulate among themselves a compatible working relationship. Our mutual objective, always, was integrity of the system. This simply meant creating a true family identity for Holiday Inns.

(Today, incidentally, franchising has evolved into something quite different, with parent companies becoming greedy and dictatorial, and imposing disgracefully unilateral contracts on the franchise holder that no business person with a sense of self-worth should sign without protest.)

You don't want to be burdened with details of the contractual fine print that I eventually drew up. We lawyers love fine print, you know! But I can tell you what happened when it was presented for adoption.

The convening of franchisees, which I so dreaded, could not be put off any longer. In April 1956 we invited all of them to come to company headquarters in Memphis—only we arranged to meet on slightly more upgraded premises than Rayner Street, in an empty room in a commercial building Kemmons owned. The night before, we treated them all to a fine dinner and a few speeches. But I left early when the realization hit me that I still had to put the constitution and by-laws into their final polished form.

It took me until the wee hours of the morning to get my job done and run off copies on the old mimeograph machine, but by meeting time it was ready for distribution. A thorough presentation was made, and I was holding my breath and crossing my fingers and praying all at the same time, in a panic of worry that some sharp-eyed man would spot a fatal flaw that would blow the whole document to pieces. There were questions and comments, of course, but nothing antagonistic was said.

At last, one of the franchisees moved adoption. Joe Vaterott of St. Louis, perhaps the most distinguished and esteemed citizen of that city at the time, had a word to say: "Gentlemen, I believe we have a contract and constitution that we can work together under, and I want to commend Bill Walton for the excellent job he has done in putting all of this together."

I hope I didn't do anything foolish at that moment, but I was so relieved that I could have danced a jig on the spot! Holiday Inns, Inc., had just become the proud parent of the National Association of Holiday Inns (which in just a few years would become international).

No longer was this the dream of one man, Kemmons Wilson, who had been infuriated with the kind of lodgings he found along the highway when he took his family on a trip, and had returned to Memphis determined to turn the industry around.

No longer was this a glowing glossary of promises that Jack and Barney had peddled as they rattled around the country in an old station wagon that still carried telltale signs and smells of its previous career as a manure-hauler!

No longer was this just a verbal agreement and a folksy handshake over some bottles of Orange Crush at a picnic. Holiday Inns, Inc., was a bona fide business enterprise, with its service mark registered with the government in Washington, its own inns ready to supply the staff training needs of the new franchisees, its attention-getting name going up on a "Great Sign" with a flashing star in several parts of the country, and all its distinctive features becoming the talk of the trade as families and business travelers discovered that these places were *different* from anything they had known before.

Thus I found out that God could cope with the modern business scene. And not only cope, but that he could still create, through human minds and imagination that turned to him for help, fresh ways of responding to human needs.

And I don't think he stopped doing that thirty years ago with the advent of Holiday Inns. It seems to me that we have never lived in an era of more exciting possibilities for proving God's faithfulness and power to work wonders in our everyday lives. He is the same yesterday, today, and forever, the Bible tells us. But "same" doesn't mean "static" where God is involved. It means "dynamic." He never changes, but he is forever making all things new—and that's in the Bible, too.

No one is locked into the past. With God, we know that to be true with regard to our salvation. Through the gift of his Son, Jesus, whose obedient death on the cross made atonement for our rebellion, our sins have been forgiven, we have been born again by the Spirit of God, we are new creatures in Christ, and as one of the great believers put it, "The future is as bright as the promises of God." At Holiday Inns, Inc., this young ex-lawyer named Bill Walton did not forget what God had done for him in answer to his prayers.

I was flattered with the compliments I got from veteran businessmen, but I did not forget to whom the credit really belonged. And when the party ended, and the franchisees went home from Memphis, I returned to my little office on Rayner Street and sat down at the slab-door desk, relieved and happy, and thankful to God.

Mostly, though, I was determined. We had a solid legal foundation now, and we had momentum building for franchise growth.

The vision was clear to me. As far as my responsibility and authority went as executive vice president, I was determined to make Holiday Inns a God-honoring company.

How little I knew!

11 ★ Building on Bedrock

What are we going to do as a corporation, and how are we going to do it?

That became the double-edged concern at the home office once the franchising crisis had been worked out. It was one thing to have a nice set of legal documents with their embossed seals and all the dignitaries' signatures in place, showing that we were a full-fledged business corporation. It was something else again to open our front door to the public and start serving their practical needs on a daily, even hourly, basis.

In some kinds of businesses, everything goes on in the offices or out on the sales floor or on the assembly line. Well, we didn't have any major problem handling the office part of it in our cubbyholes on Rayner Street. We didn't even need an intercom system; a medium-sized yell from one person could be heard by everybody in the whole headquarters complex. Communication was, shall we say, intimate and informal.

Neither were we overly anxious about what the franchisees were doing out in the field, since at that point most of them were still in the construction stage, with their Holiday Inns not even open for business yet.

True, we did have to develop an instant thirty-day

training program to live up to our promises, and to establish central control over operations. Mr. Vogel, manager of the Holiday Inn at 980 South Third Street in Memphis, was very cooperative in letting us use his staff as tutors for our original on-the-job training, with his inn as the laboratory, because he was as eager as we were to make this new approach to overnight lodging a successful breakthrough.

So I had to give high priority to the particulars of running a Holiday Inn on a day-to-day basis—finding just where everyone fit into the picture, from yardman to waitress to maid to manager. As I approached that challenge, however, one concern took higher priority.

What was to be the underlying management philosophy for implementing the Holiday Inns distinctives? What principles would shape and control our practices? I could easily draw up a list of dos and don'ts for our employees, but there had to be a "why" in back of it, a reason that would set us apart from others in the industry. Otherwise we would simply be the new kid on the block going through all the existing conventional routines, competing for customers with higher promotional pressure or fancier gimmicks.

Incidentally, I would guess that it is probably just as important for Christian organizations and churches to review once in awhile the "why" that gives them their distinctives. But I don't want to get in over my head on that subject since I'm only a layman, and I don't pretend to know how preachers think. I just sit back and let them instruct and inspire me through their sermons. What I needed was a key to the special meaning of Holiday Inns.

Philosophy of operations was not Kemmons' strong suit, shall we say. Entrepreneur that he was, he loved to start things but he hated to run them, and he often went on record as saying so. He had come up with the Holiday Inns idea in the first place because he didn't like the treatment he and his family encountered at other people's motels. He knew that he wanted more courtesies and comforts when he stayed in such places, and his instinct told him there must be thousands of other travelers who felt the same way he did. But pragmatic results were what interested him, not "reasons."

For me, as a lawyer, the "why" of a case had always mattered a lot, though of course I had to give careful consideration to the facts as well. In court, motivation was always a major focus of attention for the judge and the jury—in fact, the law recognizes motivation as the deciding factor in determining the "degree" of the crime in all kinds of situations, from murder to libel. So I was trained to poke around behind the outward appearance of things to get at the source or stimulus of an act.

The promise of making a lot of money was not what had really drawn me into Kemmons' enterprise, for one thing because immediate cash flow was next to nil, and economically I was starting under a tremendous handicap. What appealed to me about the concept was the quality of service it promised for the public. You understand well by now that I had always been obsessed by standards of quality, wanting always to be identified with the best—in my housing, in my education, in my business associations, in my friendships, in just about everything. Holiday Inns, it appeared to me, stood a real good chance of becoming the best in the business, and that is what made me want to be part of it.

If it were to reach that standard, though, I felt deeply that we needed more than superior accommodations and amenities to offer travelers at a reasonable price. We needed a driving force in everybody who worked for us that to be the "best maid," for instance, was even more important than furnishing our rooms with the "best bed."

We, the people, were to be absolutely the best the public could find anywhere in the lodging industry. But pretty uniforms wouldn't insure that. How, then, could we become the best?

I believe God gave me the answer to that fundamental question in one key word—*Attitude.* How we felt to-

ward the public was the necessary key to how we
would act toward the public.

I did a lot of heart-searching about this matter. Since
childhood I had been involved with the life of my
church in one way or another. I took the Ten Com-
mandments and the Sermon on the Mount seriously,
even though I knew without a doubt that I didn't live
up to them—and I feared the Lord partly for that
reason. I had come through life thus far without any
scandal attached to my name because I tried to be as
decent as I knew how to my family and friends and
clients.

I suddenly remembered the way young GIs had sought
me out for counseling at the Air Force Base because
they found out I had law training and I seemed older to
them than the actual five years of age at most that
separated us. They also knew, by the strictness of my
training methods, that this tough old (twenty-three)
Sarge cared about their survival when they got into the
real thing. And I would tell them what Mama had told
me, that they should not be afraid because God would
be with them. I think I might even have tried to reassure a few of them that he would surely take them
home to heaven if they died in battle. We Americans
have always been a little fuzzy in our thinking when it
comes to relating individual heroism to personal salvation, but I didn't know any better.

Drawing upon my postage stamp sized knowledge of
the Bible, I decided that the underlying management
philosophy, and corresponding employee attitude, at
Holiday Inns would be respect for the dignity of every
individual and the Christian principle of love for your
neighbor. Who could object to anything so basically
humanitarian as that? In fact, even though I used the
word "Christian," which some regarded as sectarian, I
suppose, I didn't know that Jesus was quoting the Old
Testament when he said that—so it was just as Jewish a
precept as it was Christian.

Wallace Johnson stood staunchly beside me on this
matter, because he was a devout and loyal Southern

Baptist. I don't recall that he shouted "Amen" when I first introduced the idea, but I do believe he must have said it in his heart, and meant it with all his heart. He never made any apologies for his beliefs, and he was probably the most evangelical in his expression of them in company meetings and publications since he knew chapter and verse far better than I did.

A company based on the Christian teaching of "Love thy neighbor"—that was my dream. I must confess that my understanding of Christianity didn't go much deeper than that, which was probably just as well. If I had forced some religious issue, I ran a real risk of alienating franchisees who were Jewish, Catholic, all brands of Protestant, or not adherents to any religious group at all. You can be sure I had no intention of driving any qualified inn owner out of the system over some religious hairsplitting.

That "love thy neighbor" philosophy, when linked up with our professional dedication to "the fine old innkeeping tradition in a modern setting," was bound to affect the rules and regulations that became my next major challenge: creating an Operating Manual that would spell out in detail the way to run each and every Holiday Inn on a day-to-day basis. We couldn't put anything in there, of course, that required every busboy or desk clerk to go to church on Sunday. But we could put in a whole lot of particular ways that the busboy and the desk clerk, along with everybody else including corporate officers, could demonstrate the *Attitude* to make our guests happy, and help them to think first of Holiday Inns whenever they were traveling and needed a home away from home.

Some cynic in another company wrote a note after the manual was published with the comment that it read like a Boy Scout Handbook. It was meant as an insult, of course, but I felt complimented that our message had come through so clearly! It illustrates, however, that anyone who takes a strong moral stand in this fallen world is going to be the target of ridicule and contention.

I believed in God, and I had prayed constantly for him to give me wisdom to make the right decisions, and the courage to carry them out for the glorification of his Kingdom. But to a large extent I still based my hope of heaven on doing the best I could as best I knew how—in other words, a religion of works.

Much of what I will describe about Holiday Inns practices, while they were instituted with all sincerity— and even shocked some leaders in business that we could "get away" with them—may not have pleased the Lord as much as I assumed they did because they sprang from my "works" mentality. My subconscious rationale may have been something like this: I was a good guy because I did so many good things for God, and he would find me acceptable to him on that basis.

Let me jump ahead of the story for a minute to illustrate how I was taught a lesson in the impossibility of building a Christian company as I conceived it. Project your thinking to the early 1970s. At least sixteen years have now passed since those dismal beginnings on Rayner Street. The modern business miracle of Holiday Inns has moved to the top of the industry, with more guest rooms available than all our closest competitors combined; we have 150,000 employees; revenues are edging up toward the $2 billion mark; I have been promoted from executive vice president to president of the corporation, second in command and still chief operating officer.

The executive committee is in session on the fourth floor at headquarters in Holiday City on Lamar Avenue in Memphis, faced with a proposition for improving our bottom line situation. Believe me, officers and directors are always looking for ways to improve that bottom line of profit to please shareholders and excite the security analysts.

Pay-per-view, in-room movies are the latest craze coming onto the hotel scene at that moment, and certain top leaders within our company strongly advocate that we add them to Holiday Inns guest services. The plan presented in the boardroom is for a sliding scale of charges—with family type films at the minimum rate, and X-rated films topping out at something like $7. The argument is that weekend occupancy always runs lower, and this would be one way of building up trade.

You've got the picture? "Making a lot of money" was part of the founder's dream, which all the rest of us had bought into. And a whole lot of people by now had made multimillion-dollar personal fortunes through Holiday Inns franchises and shareholdings. Here's a chance to make some more.

As presiding officer at the meeting, I suppose I shouldn't have entered the discussion and just satisfied myself with preserving the detached neutrality of the "chair." But I knew the kind of traffic we would be attracting for the weekends, and it violated my principles of decency. For the price of a room plus the $7 variety of movie, we would pull in a bunch of prostitutes and their johns, or husbands cheating on their wives and vice-versa, and turn our company ideal of "fireside human relations" into "hot pillow" orgies.

I said all that in the meeting, adding: "You want to turn Holiday Inns into the biggest whorehouses on the highways!" I wasn't whispering.

You can be sure that "polite discussion" goes out the window when the debate gets that heated, and corporate officers—pin-striped suits and all—degenerate into nothing different from common street brawlers. When we finally got orderly enough to take the vote, the motion was defeated.

One officer immediately stormed out of the room, bellowing at me, "Do you realize you have just cost this company possibly $7 million of income?" He slammed the door behind him so hard that he split a piece of the trim.

Later, Wallace stopped by my office for a little heart-to-heart talk.

"Why did you do that, Bill?" he asked in his gentle drawl, his heavy jowls waggling as he shook his head. "You were chairman of the committee, and you didn't have to vote at all unless there had been a tie. You are just putting your position in jeopardy by not refraining from getting into those squabbles."

Even my personal secretary, Eunice Bailey, the epitome of discretion, who took minutes in the executive committee meeting, forsook her customary professional reserve on that occasion and asked me demurely later in the privacy of my office if I thought it was wise to antagonize a fellow officer to that extent.

So much for "love thy neighbor"! (I wonder what the carpenter thought who had to come in and repair the splintered door.)

I think we made the right decision on that issue, and that God approved. Since then, of course, such in-room movies have become practically universal in the hotel business, and whenever it was that Holiday Inns voted them in, I have no idea because I wasn't around any longer by then. But why did I take my moral stand in such an immoral manner?

I'm sure the Lord didn't look kindly on the venomous feelings I harbored toward fellow officers who had voted in favor of the motion. I can only say that every time some argument or debate like that came up—whether in committee or board meetings, or in a one-on-one with Kemmons in his office—some urge to resist seemed to well up within me automatically. I didn't have any self-control over the position I was taking. I would be into a heated argument before I knew it, and instead of backing down and getting out of it gracefully I would hang onto the issue and snarl over it like a bulldog over a piece of meat.

Was it my Christian convictions or just a stubborn streak? Was I honestly thinking of the public good, or was I merely determined to have things go my way by flaunting my administrative clout? Or, is it possible that it is one way the Holy Spirit works in some of us short-fuse folks to help us "fight the good fight of faith" the Bible talks about?

I can't answer those questions any better today looking back than I could at the time they were first asked of me. Who among us can ever be sure of our motives? I can only say this: to my way of thinking, principle dictated practice at Holiday Inns from the day I finished putting together that Operating Manual. It stood like Gibraltar as the guidebook of the corporation, which I was willing to fight for in any way necessary to preserve the integrity of the system.

The liquor situation was another case. In high school and college I avoided the social drinking scene, probably tracing my aversion back to childhood and the unhappy situation in my family life, which I attributed mainly to liquor. We absolutely ruled beverage alcohol off all Holiday Inns premises in our initial charter. But a modification of that policy kind of "sneaked" in gradually, with strict limitations on where and how it was to be served (beer and wine only, at first). In fact, the introduction was so subtle and minimal that insiders jokingly referred to the "Wallace Johnson bars" because he was an adamant teetotaler who had wholeheartedly supported their exclusion from the start. With the passage of years, though, an occcasional amendment now and then finally made the bar a big social center at an inn, and I guess the records would show that I voted "Yes" on the question.

Inconsistent of me? Yes. Don't ask me why. Years later, at a major Christian gathering in Dallas in 1972, someone who was attending my businessmen's seminar demanded to know how a man of my convictions could let my company become the world's largest bar operator. By then it was an accepted fact of life at Holiday Inns, and I had no defense or justification that would satisfy such a challenger.

To me, "love your neighbor," as Jesus taught it, was meant to be the outworking demonstration of one's love for God. I took it that seriously, especially where our company employees and our inn guests were concerned. If there was one place where I was vulnerable to breaking that commandment, it seems to have been in the disagreeable way I fought out my disagreements with my fellow officers and board members.

Was it that I held some grudge toward them and felt an ill-willed urge to put them down? Was it because I was hurt and disillusioned that they couldn't seem to understand how we were undercutting our own integrity by changing policies in such a way as to contradict or even to repudiate our chartered principles? Or was it nothing more than that red-headed people tend to be scrappers?!

TOP: (l. to r.)
William B. Walton I
William B. Walton III
(my father)
William B. Walton II

BOTTOM: Katherine
Walters Walton (my
mother and me in
1920; I was six
months old)

TOP: My graduation from law school in 1941 following years of night classes

BOTTOM: I was Number 1 in the draft. Mr. Roosevelt pulled my number out.

'That's My Number'---They're First In Draft Lottery

TOP: My bride, Geneva Chase, and me on our wedding day, October 21, 1944

BOTTOM: Five generations on my mother's side of the family: my mother and me, my grandmother, William Jr., and my great-grandmother (age 100)

TOP: Our first planning meeting: (l. to r.) Wallace E. Johnson, Bill Walton, Kemmon Wilson

MIDDLE: Holiday Inn General Offices at 877 Rayner Street in Memphis (1956)

BOTTOM: Holiday Inn's first day on the New York Stock Exchange. I'm on the left. The two men in the center are Wilson and Johnson.

TOP: With Bob Hope; It was not all work!

BOTTOM: Billy Graham introduces Bill Walton at the 1978 Memphis Mid South Billy Graham Crusade

TOP: President Nixon with Bill Walton; Billy Graham looking on

MIDDLE: (l. to r.) Bud James, CEO of Sheraton Corp.; Senator Hubert Humphrey; Bill Walton. Good friends, sharing the platform in San Juan, Puerto Rico

BOTTOM: Howard Baker and Bill Walton; a couple of Tennesseans on the Washington front

TOP: A conference with President Ford in the Roosevelt Room at the White House

CENTER: With President Jimmy Carter

BOTTOM: Bill and Geneva Walton, enjoying fellowship with a friend, Senator Daniel Inouye

TOP: Bill Walton addressing the World Travel and Tourism Conference at the Hague, hosted by the Netherlands

BOTTOM: Bill Walton and Bill Marriot in Moscow, part of President Ford's Trade Mission to Russia (note: bottles are Russian fruit juice!)

The Walton Family at
Glen Echo (1986)

Scenes at
our home,
Glen Echo

TOP RIGHT: The Walton Family on the *Glen Echo Queen*, on Lake Geneva

TOP: The Holiday Inn Chapel on the grounds of Forsythe, Georgia; a "Walton Years Program"

BOTTOM: The *Glen Echo Queen* in front of the Lake House on Lake Geneva

Springtime at Glen
Echo

TOP: Bill Walton at new inn job site

BOTTOM: Grand Opening

TOP: Bill Walton,
Ruth Graham, Billy
Graham and Geneva
Walton at Bill Wal-
ton's study at Glen
Echo

BOTTOM: A scene in
the gate house of the
new Walton Hotel
Corporation inn

TOP: The Walton
Hotel Corp. President
and Vice-President
(Bill and Geneva)
build an Inn of their
own for a change.

BOTTOM: Bill and
coauthor Melvin Lor-
entzen at Glen Echo
working on books

12 ★ All You Can Do Is Try

Motives for action are a hard thing to analyze because none of us is perfect, and our motives are always mixed. I guess I thought, at least some of the time, that I was fighting God's battles for him at Holiday Inns, not realizing that he probably was capable of handling his own defense better than I was.

But, back to the beginnings. Those bitter and bombastic confrontations were not the normal order of proceedings, especially in the first fifteen years or so, when the phenomenal expansion of the company was astonishing the business world and the financial markets. After all, with such remarkable reports coming to the board constantly on the current state of the balance sheets, we were a pretty jubilant and jovial bunch most of the time. We had a lot to cheer about, even to crow about. I think the reason is obvious. We were treating people right.

Yes, it is as simple as that. We didn't have *customers* at Holiday Inns; we had *guests*. All the staff were trained rigorously to treat the families and business travelers who stayed with us, or who ate in our restaurants, with the same courtesy and attentiveness to their comfort and happiness that they would lavish on cherished visitors to their own homes. In some ways, because we were institutionalized to a reasonable degree, we might have been even more fussy about some housekeeping details than the average homemaker has time or energy to take care of, and of course housecleaning was a daily requirement at Holiday Inns.

I know we didn't score 100 percent. Complaints could occur at any inn any day, and more than a few disgruntled guests told us off in no uncertain terms through their letters to the home office. But we never let up emphasizing the *Attitude* as indispensable to our success.

Once the Operating Manual was completed, we pretty well knew what we were going to do as a corporation and how we were going to do it. That sounds simple to say, but to accomplish it meant never-ending training and inspection. And inspection routines at Holiday Inns had some peculiarities.

One thing a guest always found easily in a room at a Holiday Inn was the Gideon Bible. Why? Because we took it out of the dresser drawer and put it on top of the bedside table, and opened it! Every day the housekeeper doing daily rounds had to check for that Bible to be in place and open, just as strictly as the bathroom check for soap.

Rumors went around that I dictated what passage of Scripture the Bible should be open to. Not true. But if you have had occasion to stay in hotel and motel rooms, you know that something lying open is much more likely to attract your attention than something closed that you have to pick up and open yourself.

Motels may appear pleasant and peaceful on the outside, as they should. Inside, though, they frequently house desperate men and women. I would totally deceive myself if I thought Holiday Inn's or any other hotel's guest rooms were not sites for clandestine deals, illicit sexual affairs, rapes, suicides, and murders.

That is a sordid catalog, and it is by no means complete. But not everyone who gets caught up in life's tangles is satisfied to accept the situation. Many are looking for a way out so that they can keep going, but they don't know who to turn to among their family members or friends. When they check in at a motel, they often are ashamed, or running scared, or both.

My files hold scores, if not hundreds, of letters from guests over the years who bothered to write and say how helped they were, upon entering their room, to look down on that open Bible and read the first thing to meet their eye, whatever the section might be.

Some people felt that the Lord must have arranged the "coincidence" of the verses addressing the very need in their life at that moment.

A few of the stories are dramatic—of suicides prevented, of marriages preserved, of guidance for important decisions, or of comfort in a crisis. The Word of God does not return void, we read. If the Book of Books stays in a drawer in a motel, or if it stays on the shelf in our homes, it doesn't get a fair chance to bring to us the spiritual message that can save the day—or save a soul.

My open Bible policy raised a storm in some religious quarters, of all places. The Roman Catholics and the Mormons protested in particular, at one time to the point of even threatening litigation. I sat down with their respective authorities and explained that if I were to stock every motel room with representative sectarian literature, I would have to put in library shelves to hold it all. They saw my point and good-naturedly agreed that a Bible by itself was the safest compromise.

(It interests me, by the way, that because of the owners' religious persuasion, all Marriott hotel rooms contain the Book of Mormon as well as the Gideon Bible. I'm not the only businessman, by a long shot, who wants to offer spiritual guidance along with other services. Cecil Day, when he founded his highly successful Day's Inns system, activated a chaplain-on-call program.)

I am thankful to the Lord for the Gideons, and for those two traveling businessmen who met in a Wisconsin hotel in 1898 and caught the vision of supplying the lodging industry with copies of God's Word at no charge—extending their work eventually to schools, hospitals, prisons, and other institutions in more than a hundred countries. It has been what we often describe as a "silent witness," but where the Word of God is open, an open mind and heart will hear the voice of God—and that has happened hundreds of thousands of times in the Holiday Inns system worldwide, thanks to the diligence of business and professional laymen and women who bear the noble name of Gideons.

I can't resist adding a footnote to that word of appreciation. Only when the records are opened in eternity will we know how many people have found Christ by reading a Gideon Bible in a hotel room. If the organization had gotten ambitious to branch out into all kinds of other ministries, instead of keeping their priority on Scripture distribution, I think the results would be diminished. They have good business sense.

In business there is a practice we call diversification, through which a company doing a certain kind of business acquires, in one way or another, companies engaged in other kinds of businesses, sometimes closely related, sometimes very different.

The common explanation is the wisdom of the old proverb not to put all your eggs in one basket. The resulting conglomerates, as they are known in today's marketplace, are almost mind-boggling. We just can't keep track anymore of who owns whom, and who's doing or making or offering what.

At Holiday Inns, we surely experienced both the dazzling and the dismal sides of this phenomenon. As the company grew rapidly, with the number of inns seeming to multiply almost overnight, we not only had to provide training and inspection, but in order to maintain quality control as part of the system we had to help with site selection, construction, interior decorating, furnishing and equipping, advertising and promotion, and food service. In some cases, we were such heavy purchasers from certain vendors that it paid both them and us simply to take them over as

Holiday Inns subsidiaries so that they could supply us exclusively. In other cases, no vendor could meet the size of our orders, so we had to create our own internal subdivision as supplier. In fact, we became so good at producing certain things that we actually became a supplier to others in our own industry.

All of that is a legitimate part of the growth pattern, although it takes sound managerial judgment to decide which option is the best stewardship. Along with every move like that, also, come new needs for workers and supervisors and administrators, for offices and facilities, and for communications and distribution systems. Company operations become more elaborate and complex. In a growth phase like that, the area of administration is where some of the more serious breakdowns occur.

Let me put in a good word for the churches here. A lot of them are experiencing remarkable growth today. We who are laymen when it comes to theology can offer our spiritual leaders the insights and managerial skills God has given us as part of our contribution to their cause.

For a number of years it has been my privilege to serve on the board of the Billy Graham Evangelistic Association, whose worldwide operations in the Minneapolis headquarters, strictly from my point of view as a business executive, have been excellently managed by George Wilson through all these decades until his recent retirement.

I know that all kinds of offers have come Billy's way to get involved in other things, from education to politics. But one of the things I admire most about him is that unswerving single-mindedness with which he devotes himself to evangelism. He believes that is his gift from God, and that it is the one ministry on which he should concentrate his full energy. He has held to that for forty years!

Preaching the gospel is his calling, so he does only that, whether it is through crusades, radio, television, films, books, or magazine. I don't think I know anyone,

in church work or in business, who has limited himself
with more consistency, and I admire Billy a great deal
for that.

I say that not as a religious expert or a Bible scholar,
because I'm neither one. I say it as a business executive
who had to learn that lesson for myself the hard way.
And, I repeat, we who have some degree of expertise in
our own fields ought to be more available to counsel
spiritual leaders on business matters for the sake of the
Kingdom.

Holiday Inns was founded for the hospitality business.
In order to meet our intrinsic requirements, we legiti-
mately developed sources for specialized services,
internally or externally, to enhance the hospitality business. But the day came, as we prospered in doing
what we knew best how to do, when ambition clouded
our common sense and we found ourselves owning bus
companies and steamship lines and even a South
American rain forest. When we paired up with gasoline
companies and credit card companies, we basically got
ourselves into all kinds of arrangements and align-
ments that almost drained the coffers dry.

The result was that we had bought or borrowed so
much trouble administratively we couldn't look after
our priority, the hospitality business, the way we
should have. Our reputation began slipping, and our
revenues dropped.

What was behind all that? I'm going to oversimplify
my answer to a question that is highly complex by
saying just this: We lost the *Attitude.* Saving the corporation became a higher priority than serving the public.

I wanted to honor God in my management of the
company by giving him the credit for the miracle that
eventually happened, taking us to the top of the heap.
But when we got there, something happened to me. I
could have the company Lear jet at my disposal to fly
me where I wanted when I wanted, and innkeepers all
over the world rolled out the red carpet to welcome
me. The press clipping files bulged with news and
feature stories of our phenomenal success, and awards

and honors began to flow in from the industry and the community. Even the heads of state of foreign countries came to Holiday City in Memphis to see firsthand this commercial miracle. When all this happened, do you know what Bill Walton was thinking to himself, and maybe even saying out loud more than he meant to? *"My company!"*

The reason I know that was the case is that today, a dozen years after moving up from president to vice chairman of the board, and now in retirement, you will still hear me talk about Holiday Inns as *"my company!"*

In the beginning, I had prayed, "Lord, help me. You know I can't do this job on my own. Help me run these operations for your glory."

"My company!"

Call it empire building, call it ego feeding, call it whatever you want to. It is simply taking to ourselves the credit that belongs only to the Lord. I did it, and I'm ashamed that I did it, and I still need divine help to get it out of my system.

Ego trips are the costliest traveling you can do in this life.

They destroy other people, and they dispute the lordship of Jesus Christ.

Jesus told about a Pharisee praying in the temple, a religious leader who was on an ego trip if anybody ever was. Imagine saying to God, who knows all about us, "I thank you that I am not like other men." So "spiritual" he was proud of it!

Do you think it is easy for an executive in any organization to say—and mean it—like the tax collector in the same story, "I am a sinner"? The ego trip is over the minute we look at Jesus.

We did other official things at Holiday Inns to demonstrate that we cared about more than just the physical comfort of our guests. It wasn't enough to make sure the light bulbs worked in every lamp in a room, or even that the Gideon Bible was open on the table. I knew from the close contact that I maintained with our innkeepers across the country that a lot of them found themselves with troubled guests on their hands, needing someone to pour out their woes to. Bartenders meet a lot of people like that, too, strangers who feel safe confiding in strangers, and whose inhibitions have been relaxed by liquor. You may have sat beside someone like that on a plane flight, someone who told you all about his family or personal crisis because he didn't have anybody else who would listen.

Although it wasn't widespread business practice, I knew that there existed a very rare breed of ministers called "industrial chaplains," who served as counselors to employees. I arranged for us to provide that employee benefit at Holiday Inns by hiring the Rev. W. A. "Dub" Nance, a Methodist minister with a record of effective parish ministry, to be company chaplain. His responsibilities included counseling, visiting the sick, comforting the bereaved, sending birthday greetings or messages of cheer, writing occasional editorials for the company house organ, and similar pastoral duties.

We were not trying to be a church in the business world. But a lot of our employees were not church-going folks, and when some blow struck they didn't know where to turn for help. Besides, the presence of a company chaplain reinforced that *Attitude* of "love your neighbor" and communicated a wordless message to everybody that company management didn't use such terminology idly.

Through Dub's efforts we reached out to the whole system with the chaplain-on-call program. In every local community where there was a Holiday Inn, we sought to recruit one or more ministers who would volunteer to respond to a guest who needed spiritual help.

We knew they all had plenty of demands from their own parishioners, as well as leadership commitments both inside and outside the church. Yet, being the selfless kind of servants to the Lord that they are, they were willing to volunteer.

In each room, then, a little tent card on the table gave the name and phone number of a minister who would be available for counsel. We weren't trying to get a reputation as some kind of religious asylum for kooky tourists, but as a business that cared about our guests' emotional and spiritual needs as well as physical ones.

It was not an evangelism program. We were not trying to convert people, or to proselytize them for a certain faith. True, some people did come into a redemptive relationship with God under a chaplain's counsel. Others simply got the spiritual or psychological shot in the arm they needed to get through the lonely night, and then went on their way the next morning, never to be heard from again.

Sometimes the calls represented critical emergencies— like someone dying, or threatening suicide, or being grief-stricken by some message of a tragedy back home that they found waiting for them when they checked in at the Holiday Inn. At its peak, this program enlisted the unselfish assistance of nearly two thousand local ministers.

Those men were not out to get members for their churches, because they knew the calls from Holiday Inns were from folks just passing through. They were not "too busy," even, to talk to someone who was experiencing no greater crisis than homesickness or loneliness, and just needed someone to visit with for a few minutes, even over the phone.

I have to say, sadly, that chaplains' efforts to help were sometimes to no avail, and human tragedy relentlessly ran its course. But again, letters of gratitude from travelers who encountered a caring local minister through the Holiday Inn program filled our files. The innkeepers themselves wrote frequently to say what a relief it was for them to have an expert in emotional and spiritual problems take the burden off their shoulders, especially since they had other important duties to discharge in running the inn.

Although many people condemned us for the open Bible policy and the chaplain program, including some ministers, who charged us with trying to start "motel religion" across the country, I don't remember hearing of any guest who canceled a reservation or walked out on us because of it. And I believe that the Final Day of Reckoning is going to find a good many people rejoicing in the presence of the Lord because of it.

The caring attitude has become increasingly rare in business today. How many stores can you go into anymore with a clerk saying, "How may I help you?" As often as not they say, "Did you want something?" as if to suggest that they have no time for you unless you are a potential spender.

And what is the meaning of the word "waiter" in a restaurant? You can sit for a half-hour trying to catch their eye or flag them down or trip them or something, when they are supposed to be "waiting" to respond to your needs.

We all know how irritating that can be. That is why part of the Holiday Inns Operating Manual procedure indicated, for example, that the desk clerk would not answer a room phone call curtly with "Front desk" but rather with a warm "May I help you?"

Such caring costs. Sometimes inconvenience. Sometimes discomfort. Sometimes money, or time, or energy—or prayer. But caring is what people need and value, so it is good for every business. At Holiday Inns there were people in high position in the company who fought me tooth and nail on some of the policies I have been describing. You can imagine how they felt when I initiated a weekly prayer breakfast. A prayer meeting at midweek on the premises of the corporation can be a dandy deterrent to hypocrisy.

You can't expose each other to the Word of God, and then pray to the Lord in each other's hearing, without realizing—at least during the moment of truth—that you will have to "put up or shut up" on the job.

I found the prayer breakfasts at Holiday Inns to be mighty challenging to my own faith, in the simple way that business executives tend to look at things. I believed God was guiding me, because I asked him to, and that he was prospering Holiday Inns, because I was trying to please him.

I introduced the prayer breakfast idea into the annual

conference of the National (later International) Holiday
Inns Association, our couple of thousand franchisees
and their innkeepers. The first year I tried one, 1966,
our speaker was Dr. Norman Vincent Peale, and everybody was suitably inspired by that renowned positive
thinker. The next year Dr. Billy Graham recorded a
message for us, and then in 1968 he came in person at
my invitation to be the speaker, and we had an
overflow crowd. As always, though his remarks were
entirely appropriate to the occasion and the audience,
Billy didn't miss his chance to convey the essence of
the gospel very clearly. He was well received.

How well? One of our pioneer and major franchise
holders, a Jew, made a motion that every member of
the Holiday Inns system, including the company itself,
chip in $100 each for the good work Dr. Graham was
doing.

He made return engagements, and we had a variety of
other inspirational speakers. The franchisees, whatever
their religion or irreligion, seemed to regard the opening prayer breakfast as a major highlight of each year's
conference.

All the time, though, I was becoming more and more
unsure of the future of the company. That breathtaking
rise from below bottom to industry leader in fifteen
years had produced a corporation with growing personality tensions and policy disagreements. It was
bound to happen, even though I, in romantic optimism,
assumed the presidency in 1969 fully confident that
our best years were ahead of us.

Certainly we had proved that our philosophy of respect for individual dignity and love for neighbor had
won us public support and industry acclaim unprece-
dented in our profession. Two billion dollars gross on
the bottom line was hard evidence.

The climb up Success Mountain had been thoroughly
exhilarating for me up to this point, exceeding my
dreams. I looked forward and upward to scaling new
heights. Wallace, unfortunately, had become too ill for
us realistically to expect him to carry his accustomed

duties, so he was moved up to vice chairman of the board. Kemmons held his grip on the chairmanship as chief executive officer, and moved me up to president, succeeding Wallace.

Congratulations poured in from all over the world. It was mighty heady stuff for a boy from a broken home with a night school law degree. I could even catch enticing glimpses of the chairmanship for myself when there was a break in the thickening clouds at the top.

But contrary to expectations, *my company* was heading into its worst years, not its best. I was not alert to the treacherous slopes on the last few meters of the climb to the summit. I did not know how swiftly a deadly storm could sweep a man away at that altitude.

13 ★ Bankrupt

"Mr. Walton's emotional attachment to Holiday Inns appears to cloud his business judgment."

That terse entry in Miss Bailey's journal in November 1979 spoke volumes. Was I approaching my silver anniversary year with Holiday Inns, Inc., the company I loved and had lived for, only to lose my grip on myself and my footing on the mountain?

Some success story!

"Stay in there and hang on as long as you can," my friend Billy Graham counseled me.

"Keep fighting the battle, but don't get into theological arguments in the boardroom," advised another wise clergyman.

Had Holiday Inns, Inc., collapsed? Was it a takeover target for some greedy conglomerate? Did management sense impending disaster?

Quite the contrary. A feature story in the *New York Times* on Sunday, August 5, 1979, with the by-line of Barbara Lovenheim, was headed: HOLIDAY INNS IS BOOMING. That was only three months before Miss Bailey's comment about my "emotional attachment."

In the *Times* story, the brand new president, Michael D. Rose, thirty-seven years old and the second man to succeed me in that position in five years, was quoted as saying: "The company outgrew a lot of people and their talents. . . . There's no one from the old group left."

A slight error of fact in that last statement. I, a co-founder of Holiday Inns back when Mike Rose was twelve years old, was still "left," wearing the title of vice chairman of the board since my "elevation" from the presidency in 1974, and representing the company and the industry in Washington, D.C., on extremely vital matters affecting tourism and the United States government.

Why, then, should I give the appearance of being so distressed that Miss Bailey was moved to record the clouding of my business judgment? Gradually, I will unfold the answer to that question, but I'll satisfy your curiosity right now by putting the situation in just four words: Holiday Inns was bankrupt!

Not financially, of course. "Booming" was the right word in that newspaper headline, with certain revenue centers in the company showing tremendous increases in profits.

The bankruptcy was moral. "For the good of the business," in the words of my presidential successor before he retired, Holiday Inns, like Faust, had made a Mephistophelean (that's a fancy word for "devilish") deal for rejuvenation by entering the lucrative gambling casino business.

"Fireside human relations" were transferred to the gaming table, and the "home away from home" had become a place for wage earners to part with their earnings, their savings, their possessions, and their peace. The Gideon Bible was back in the drawer, the chaplains were no longer on call, the prayer breakfasts had become "fellowship" breakfasts, and, in Mike Rose's words quoted in the *New York Times,* "The most significant development at Holiday has been the metamorphosis of the management there from entrepreneurial to professional."

A newspaper columnist on the opposite coast, Milt Moskowitz of the *San Francisco Chronicle,* probably saw through all the hoopla most accurately and summed up the situation best in his column, "Money Tree" (September 8, 1979): "Holiday Inns, the greatest lodging chain ever built, is turning its back on some principles held dearly by its founders—and everyone is applauding. . . . So Holiday Inns is out of buses and into slot machines. In the big casino, the New York Stock Exchange, the players couldn't be happier."

Well, that's what Kemmons had promised: "Some people are going to make a lot of money out of this venture." They did!

But it wasn't Bill Walton. And it wasn't the common working people who kept on coming by the busloads to the Holiday Inns casinos in Las Vegas, and Reno, and Atlantic City, and Lake Tahoe—and then went home to their families, broke.

According to news reports, operations are underway for Holiday Inns, now renamed Holiday Corporation, to add another chip to its pile of winnings by constructing the largest indoor gambling casino in the world, measuring 125,000 square feet, in Sydney, Australia.

What happened? This is not the place, nor is it my purpose, to "expose" the maneuvering, manipulation, and man-killing pressures that always are present in a catastrophe of such proportions. I will simply make a few points as I see them in my limited human perspective, and then leave the judgment to God, who alone is altogether righteous.

I'll have to retrace the steps.

On September 20, 1969, the Holiday Inns board of directors elected me president of the company, replacing Wallace Johnson, who was moved up to vice chairman of the board. A month later at the franchise owners' annual conference, my keynote speech received a standing ovation, and Kemmons Wilson told the conference how proud Holiday Inns was to have me as president. (That is not merely my recollection. It is Miss Bailey's record, to which she added: "It was a very inspiring moment.")

I am telling this to you now not to boast, but so that

you can put later developments in perspective and understand, perhaps, why my emotions couldn't be kept out of the picture. In only nine years, everything would be reversed.

The presidency of a major corporation is a seat of power. Inasmuch as I had been chief operating officer since my first day on the job in 1956, there was not much alteration in my performance, but my prerogatives were far greater, and I suppose in some people's eyes the prestige factor went up a notch or two.

Kemmons and Wallace always had allowed me to function on a long leash, so my administrative habits were firmly in place and familiar to everybody. But I was able to call at least some of the shots with more authority, and with Wallace sick and Kemmons often out of town, I had the executive reins in hand.

When a person, man or woman, gets into a spot like that, the adrenaline flow turns into a flood that makes them feel like they can attempt and achieve almost anything. "Little Boss" who had started the long climb forty years before on a newspaper route was "Boss" now, and the move to "Big Boss" wasn't very far down the hall.

I was by no means alone, however. You could never have fit on our letterhead the names of all the senior vice presidents, and vice presidents, and division directors, and other top management persons we had, reproduced many times over at the middle management level and below. We had brought them in from all over the country and had "trained them up in the way they should go"—respecting the Holiday Inns *Attitude.*

Perhaps the choicest plum the presidency gave me was opportunity to implement my longtime dream of building a Holiday Inn University where our training program could be conducted and expanded in an ideal setting with state-of-the-art educational methods and tools. Nothing impressed me as more important than to instill the *Attitude* into coming generations of innkeepers and corporate leaders. I was fifty now, and fit for another fifty years, but I knew the time would come when I would have to pass the baton to someone else. Several young men in the upper echelons of leadership were potential candidates, and I coached them, challenged them with project responsibilities, and channeled their gifts for communication into public representation of the company at several significant meetings and conferences.

It would not have been right for me to develop Bill Walton clones all over the place, because their leadership years would encounter different circumstances and crises than I had known. What would see them through then was not the way I did it but the way I saw it. The *Attitude:* respect for the individual and love for your neighbor. That is the fundamental, the bedrock, on which they would build a life and a career according to patterns that seemed best to them.

This does not obstruct development and progress. I seldom objected to operational changes that were introduced at Holiday Inns, or even to many of the policy changes, as long as none of them contradicted or counteracted the *Attitude.* We could reorganize our corporate structure to our heart's content, and introduce all kinds of variations into the format of inn construction or decor, just so long as none of those innovations diluted the name of Holiday Inns, which we had so painstakingly registered with the government as our service mark at the outset.

I never forgot Mr. Bayol's counsel about diligence. Was it possible, though, that my quarrel with gambling was personal bias and not God's view? I sought out my trusted friend Dr. Adrian Rogers, senior minister of one of the largest churches in the country, Bellevue Baptist in Memphis, who was elected president of the 15-million-member Southern Baptist Convention in 1986.

"Bill," he said, "explicit prohibition of gambling by name isn't in the Bible. But Paul warns in his Epistle to the Romans not to cause our brother to stumble, or to do anything that would offend him, or to take advantage of his weakness." Adrian helped me see clearly that gambling cannot be pleasing to the Lord. The

Tenth Commandment, "Thou shalt not covet . . . any thing that is thy neighbor's," surely must include his money, too.

That was enough substantiation to put some starch in my backbone. Within the boundaries of the *Attitude,* I saw gambling, then, as nothing more than exploitation of our base human instinct to get something for nothing, or at least to get a lot for a little, and always at the expense of someone else.

When you put your quarter in the slot machine and hit the jackpot, or when you buy your state lottery ticket at the grocery store and become that week's instant millionaire, whose money are you walking away with? Not the casino's, and not the supermarket's or the state's. You're taking for yourself, without any effort and with almost no investment, somebody else's paycheck or savings account or worse.

The term "legalized gambling" could just as well be "legalized stealing."

All of that leaves untouched the related enterprises surrounding the gambling industry. This is so well known to the American public that it is assumed to be "normal." Yet none of us think it is normal for our homes to be broken into and our family heirlooms stolen. That incident we report to the police, and we press charges if the thieves are caught, and we demand justice by the restitution of our losses.

Losers at the gambling table have no legal recourse to get it back. And winners have no legal requirement to give it back.

That was the seething crisis at Holiday Inns during my presidency from 1969 to 1973 that erupted into the obliteration of a dream that had become a dependable reality. We were a company dedicated to serving the traveling public—that was our charter.

Now forces were at work both inside and outside the company dedicated to snookering the public. But as I said earlier, I was unable or unwilling to give adequate heed to the danger signals, because I still had my original determination and drive to be the best in the industry, and the University was my idea for insuring that. So, preoccupied with a fresh dream, I didn't adequately investigate for the fire where there was smoke.

Furthermore, in 1969 none of us guessed what the Arab cartel was going to do to world commerce through their oil embargo four years later. The OPEC plot would wreak havoc with Holiday Inns stock values, personally affecting me in a calamity from which I would never recover.

Isn't it fortunate that the Lord keeps the future hidden from us? If we knew ahead of time what was coming we would probably be so super-paralyzed or super-galvanized that we would be no good to anybody. As it is, we trust him for our salvation, and we trust him for our security, and we trust him for our survival when the test comes—and go on about our daily business with good cheer.

One of the things I surely didn't anticipate happened in April 1971 in Lexington, Kentucky. If it hadn't happened, I might not be alive today.

14 ★ Saved—But Almost Destroyed

In February 1971, with a ringing in my ears that
wouldn't stop, my doctor had sent me to Florida for a
rest, encumbered with oxygen tanks, which I had to
use every two hours. While we were there, we happened to run into Billy Graham and had our first
chance to develop a personal acquaintance with him.
Ever since we had casually met when he came to speak
at our annual conference prayer breakfast in Memphis
in 1968, Geneva and I had been impressed by his fer-
vent commitment to his calling. The way God brought
us together in Florida is another illustration of that divine sense of humor!

A gray Oldsmobile pulled in just behind our car under
the portico of Earl Padgett's Holiday Inn at Vero Beach,
where we were staying. I didn't pay any attention until
the driver hopped out and hailed me. It took me a
minute to recognize that it was Dr. T. W. Wilson, an associate evangelist with the Billy Graham organization,
whose home is in Montreat, North Carolina.

T.W., as everyone calls him, is one of the world's
friendliest fellows. I remembered from those Memphis
visits that he was always ready with a homespun yarn
that put everybody in a good mood. At the time,

though, I knew little except that he was the right-hand man to the best known evangelist in modern times. I was nothing but an innkeeper, but they were hobnobbers with the high and mighty as they went about their special calling to preach the gospel.

"Bill," T.W. said after we had exchanged greetings, "this is Billy's car. I'm just about to drive over to Melbourne and meet him at the little airport where he's coming in on a plane. Why don't you ride along with me?" It was one of those invitations a man would be stupid to refuse, though I would wonder a little later whether I had been all that smart to accept. Not that there was anything wrong with T.W.'s driving or his company, but the eagerly accepted chance to meet again with Billy under such informal circumstances came near to being an anticlimax.

We got to the airport before he did. As he stepped out of the plane and came over to where we were with that long stride of his, he didn't greet me or even seem to notice that I was there.

Instead, his first words to T.W. were: "T., I'm sick. Take me straight to a hospital."

He looked it, too. At the moment, all I could do was tell them where the nearest hospital was located.

Once we got underway in the car, with Billy and me sitting together in the backseat, I told him that I was down in Florida for health reasons, too, under doctor's orders, in fact. You know the old saying, "Misery loves company," so hearing about my problem seemed to help a little to take his mind off his own.

My doctor had prescribed a mild tranquilizer to relieve stress symptoms, so I asked Billy if he would like to try one of the pills I was carrying with me. I had been listening to his recital of all the pressure he had been under just before leaving on this trip, and how they had flown down in bad weather conditions, so I figured there was probably nothing in the world wrong with him but a case of nervous exhaustion.

"Sure," he said, "give me one of those."

North Carolina country-bred as he was, Billy is such a

believer in people, trusts them so much, that he will try almost anything they prescribe. My being president of the world's largest hotel system didn't qualify me in the least to diagnose maladies or to hand out medicines, but sometimes your authority in one position seems to spill over into other areas. He reached out for the pill I offered.

"But there's no water for you to swallow it with," I protested.

"I don't need any water," he said, and gulped it down. A few minutes later, whether because of the pill or just the idea of having done something to relieve his discomfort, he seemed to brighten up.

"T.," he said, "take the turn up ahead and drive down Jungle Trail. I might as well go by and take a look at my grove." His father had given him a small acreage planted with citrus trees, and Billy built a little cabin on it that was supposed to serve as a hideaway when there was a momentary letup in his incredibly hectic international schedule. Actually, the building had been put up by one of our people and was a replica of a Holiday Inn room!

Before we reached the place, though, he spotted a familiar roadside orange juice stand run by his neighbor on his own grove, so he told T.W. to stop there. We all had some fresh chilled orange juice, and Billy had a good time chatting with his friend.

As we were about to leave, I decided to buy a bag of grapefruit to take back with me to the inn.

"Don't do that," Billy whispered to me. "We can pick them right off the trees when we get to my place."

He meant it. The minute we arrived, he hopped out of the car and headed for the nearest grapefruit tree. A ladder was leaning against it, and he started scrambling up into the branches.

"Come on, Bill!" he called.

Well, I'm short to begin with, and had put on a pretty good-sized bay window over the years, so ladder-climbing wasn't my idea of recreational exercise. But what can you do when an evangelist gives "the call"?!

I can't say I "scrambled" up behind him, but I did climb the ladder and got out on a safely sturdy branch.

Down below, T.W. shouted, "This is something I've got to get a picture of—an evangelist and a businessman climbing around in a grapefruit tree like a couple of monkeys!"

I seemed to catch a hint of blackmail in his voice! As I got to know the Graham team better, I was to find out that they were great pranksters among themselves, thinking up practical jokes to play on each other that were downright audacious at times. I'm sure that must be a significant safety valve for people whose lives are under constant public scrutiny. There is unimaginable pressure in being a celebrity of any kind, even in the field of religion I suppose. A man or woman so situated really needs a few trusted friends with whom there can be spontaneous and wholesome fun.

The two of us safely back on terra firma, and the grapefruits—picked by such illustrious though amateur hands—stowed in the trunk of the Olds, we got back on the Jungle Trail. By this time Billy was feeling so much better that I talked him into skipping the "nearest hospital" and riding back to Vero Beach, where there were excellent medical facilities available. By the time we got there, he had decided to give up the hospital option altogether, and accepted my invitation to stay at the inn. That was the beginning of a relationship I will never regret.

A month later, in March, we went back to Florida again, partly for my health, which was much better, and partly for a vacation, taking the family along. Again, Billy happened to be there, this time on a vacation with his wonderful wife, Ruth, and some of their family. We all stayed in separate suites at the Holiday Inn in Vero Beach, right on the ocean. Our acquaintance deepened into friendship.

Billy loved to jog along the beach, right at the edge of the waves, and he invited me to join him. Well, this was no more suited to a man of my girth than was climbing ladders into grapefruit trees. But I went along with his suggestion, anyway. Before we had jogged far, I sat down to rest and told him that I would be there waiting for him when he got back. I kept my word on that, as I sat panting in the hot sand and watched him lope all the way to the pier in the distance and back to me.

At mealtimes we had a favorite table in the inn's restaurant right at the ocean's edge. (After all, innkeeper Earl Padgett knew he was entertaining the president of the company!) Billy's right to privacy was seldom if ever invaded by the understanding and considerate other guests at the inn.

The intimacy of sharing our concerns and hopes created a bond between us that is all too rare among people today. Building trust in another human being takes time, and it also needs just the appropriate circumstances where the private individual can slip out from behind his public image. As president of a multi-billion-dollar international corporation, I desperately needed a friend or two like that more than I knew. In my ambitious ascent up the success mountain, I had set aside almost all of my longtime friendships to give absolute attention to building the business.

Today, so late, I realize how much it takes out of a man or woman to be constantly straining to keep up the appearance of being in control of everything going on around them. Executives seem to think they cannot expose their personal vulnerabilities or people will think they have lost their touch. They are so obsessed with that presumed burden to appear to be infallible and almighty that they set themselves up for awesome collapses. The catastrophe that strips them may be in business, or in marriage, or in family, or in health, or in fortune. But sooner or later, any person who builds a shell around himself or herself will see it crack and crumble.

The reason is simple, but people who are protecting their reputations for professional brilliance are frequently among the last to discover it. Only God is infallible and almighty. The original sin of the human race was presumption that judgment and ability were self-contained. No, they are derived. More than that, they are God-given—but only to those who are willing to admit their weaknesses, errors, and needs.

If anybody can understand "executive armor" to protect a vulnerable spot, a Christian minister can, because he knows we are sinners underneath it all. Every person in business needs a spiritual confidant. I've been fortunate to have deep friendships with pastors—Dr. Jeb Russell for many years, Dr. Adrian Rogers in my crisis time, and today Dr. Richard de Witt of Second Presbyterian Church in Memphis. They have taught me so much from pulpit and in person.

Billy Graham and I exercised more than our legs and our lungs in those quiet times together along Vero Beach back in 1971. We exercised the sacred privilege of being human with each other, both of us under the mercy and grace of God. I don't know how much that may have meant to a man of faith such as he, but to a man like me, so filled with doubts and questions, it marked the beginning of a turning point in my deliverance from self-deceiving poses. Others might have been impressed by William B. Walton, millionaire tycoon. With Billy, I was free to begin becoming an open, vulnerable, and I must add grateful, human being.

Something like that doesn't happen overnight. A man doesn't condition himself for decades to strut his stuff for public admiration and then suddenly let everybody in on his secret terrors. As I traveled all over the world telling the Holiday Inn story—an absolutely true story, and a thrilling one—I became practically homogenized into the corporation's identity. I was "The Nation's Innkeeper"; I was "Mr. Tourism," as I would get to be known in Washington in a few years. That wasn't only the way the general public and even many of my business associates saw me. It was the way I was seeing myself. It was almost as if my name had changed to "H. I. Walton."

God had surely brought this executive and that evangelist together in such rare intimacy at precisely the time I most needed to be "just plain Bill" with someone trustworthy. And Billy never pushed religion on me.

Billy told us that he was heading for an evangelistic crusade in Lexington, Kentucky, and suggested we visit it. The closest I had ever been to a religious affair of that kind was the novelty tent meeting I had set up that time for Second Presbyterian Church in Memphis. So, as much out of curiosity as out of our new friendship with Billy and Ruth Graham, in April Geneva and I flew there for the last day. Billy graciously invited me to sit on the platform.

As that final service came to its close, I watched the people filing out of their stadium seats and across the field to stand in front of the platform. Great gatherings of people always stirred me, but that night I was seated where I could look into their faces. All kinds of faces. All colors of faces. But almost all of them had one thing in common: a look of expectation in their eyes that sent tears streaming down their cheeks. My own eyes filled, and then spilled over with tears. It seemed unfitting for the president of Holiday Inns, Inc., to be weeping openly in public, but there was nothing I could do to stop it.

When a large group had gathered, Billy quietly spoke to them about the eternal importance of the decision they were registering. Like an elementary school teacher, he explained simply, step by step, what they had to acknowledge to God and accept from him. As he listed each item, I listened and responded in my own heart.

"Yes, Lord, I am a sinner."

"Yes, Lord, I do believe you sent your Son to die for my sins."

"Yes, Lord, I do want to be born again by trusting Jesus as my personal Savior."

It came with such simplicity that it sounded like nothing I had ever heard before in my whole life, in church or out. I believed. I received. I became newborn by the Spirit of God.

That "decision for Christ" did not transform me into a full-blown saint right on the spot, and the Lord is still working on that difficult project. But as I said, if that had not happened at that time in my life, I doubt very much that I could have survived those unknown perils in my path up the mountain. I went home to Memphis with a heart as full of wonderment as the shepherds must have had when they first looked on the infant Savior in the Bethlehem stable. No way could I explain in theological terms what had happened to me, but it was real—and, for me, it was a far more radical new beginning than I could have guessed.

Back home, the world did not seem to have changed, and I plunged back into routines. According to plan, Holiday Inn University did come into existence on its eighty-plus acres in northern Mississippi, right on the Tennessee border only fifteen minutes from my house. There I welcomed every incoming class, congratulated every graduating class, and was free to preach *Attitude* from morning to night, if I chose.

As every innkeeper, restaurant manager, house-keeper, and other supervisor went through the parti-cular curriculum designed for the needs of each, they were imbued not only with information and skills, not only with ideas and ideals, but with the *Attitude* plus the enthusiasm, the spirit, to carry it home and spread it like a contagion among their Inn staff. They knew, after they had been to Holiday Inn University the first time, or on repeat trips for required refresher courses, that they belonged to a great enterprise that epitomized what was meant by "service industry."

You might know I was riding high. Because we were preserving the integrity of the system by continually engendering the *Attitude* in all of our employees, we kept on seeing good financial reports from the Inn's revenue centers. What gave us headaches and ulcers, though, was the financial drain of some of our subsid-iaries. The Trailways Bus Company and Delta Steamship Lines acquisition, which we called Tco, and which as I recall cost us something like $180 million, brought us not only our first antagonistic confrontation with a union, the Teamsters, but a costly year-long strike of the bus drivers that sharply lowered revenues in that division.

That acquisition, by the way, was negotiated in principle by certain fellow officers without any consultation with me or prior reference to the executive committee and the board of directors. They broke the news to me one Sunday afternoon after I came home from church, and I became very indignant, vowing to fight it whenever it would be presented as a formal proposal for action.

Wallace phoned me later that evening to plead that I not do that, since Kemmons was determined to go ahead.

I am not going to defend my administration for the Tco fiasco, but it shows on the record that I was opposed to the merger and voted in favor of it only under pressure from other officers. I had to bear the brunt of the blame for our losses, because I was president when they happened. But we could have pulled out of even that tussle without our shirt in shreds if it had not been for the Arab cartel.

When the oil embargo hit in 1973, creating in America what we called the "energy crisis," travel plummeted and the government energy office ruled that we were a nonessential industry. Holiday Inns stock took a nosedive, from around fifty dollars to four. One of our pioneer franchisers, Roy Winegardner, who owned numerous Holiday Inns, had sold them back to the company shortly before that in exchange for stock, making him the largest single stockholder, in fact, to the tune of an estimated $40 million, and with this development he surely became the angriest stockholder.

Roy and I had been great friends ever since he first came aboard the franchise organization in the earliest years when he was a successful plumbing contractor in Missouri. I admired his style.

He knew how to use a pipe wrench, and he sure knew how to talk to a stubborn plumbing fixture! Once he became such a powerful stockholder, he was invited to sit in as an observer at executive committee meetings. I

can remember many a time when I would look over at
him from my place next to Chairman Kemmons at the
table, and we would simply shake our heads to signal
to each other our dismay and disgust with the Tco
shortfall, and an apparent mania for acquisitions by the
CEO that struck us as irresponsible.

Roy knew where the trouble spot was in Holiday
Inns, and so did I, but he told me flat out, "Bill, you
can't control it, and I can." Voting shares in a company
spell C-L-O-U-T. Roy had what he needed.

I promised to spare you the gory details, so let me
just sum up what happened. In the fall of 1973 the
board moved me up to vice chairman of the board
alongside Wallace, and put in as president a man named Ludwick M. "Lem" Clymer, who had been an account officer for the Equitable Securities Company in
Nashville that floated our first stock issue, and who was
currently our executive vice president. We were
ideological opposites, and my heart sank when that
changing of the guard came about. Solid confirmation
for my concern was going to show up in a hurry.

This move left me one-half step away from the top of
the mountain, which, by my logic, I would automatically reach when the time came eventually for Kemmons to step out in favor of his many other interests.
It might be quite a wait, though, since the man-
datory retirement age of sixty-five had been waived
by board action specifically in relation to Kemmons.
But Wallace Johnson, who had moved from president
to vice chairman three years before, would soon reach
retirement age and go on emeritus status, so there was
no one else in the "line of succession" between Kemmons and me.

Was I in for an awakening!

The time came shortly when the new president
requested a meeting with me in my home in Glen
Echo. During our lengthy discussion, after which I
made an immediate written verbatim report as my legal discipline had taught me to do, he emphatically
underscored his intentions to make some changes in

the way things were done at Holiday Inns. A lot of what he said opened my eyes at last to the inferno that had been smoldering for the past few years. The climax came as he left.

"There's no room in this company for your kind of thinking any more!" The man who succeeded me as president when I moved up to vice chairman of the board practically spat the words at me.

I seethed inside. Who did he think he was, talking to me that way?

He hadn't been at the administrative helm during those first twenty years when Holiday Inns became the largest business of its kind in the history of the world. He hadn't hovered over daily operations from kitchen to guest room to front desk to broom closet. He hadn't presided at sessions of the board and of the executive committee. He hadn't designed and directed annual meetings that brought franchisees and stockholders to their feet cheering in response to platform presentations. He hadn't flown hundreds of thousands of miles all over North America and to a score of foreign countries to preside at Inn openings. He hadn't sat with the powerful men of the Senate and Congress in Washington to hammer out legislation that brought the American tourism industry the long overdue recognition it deserved.

I had.

I had done all those things.

I had been all those places.

My kind of thinking, which he was so scornful of, wasn't the sole secret of the corporation's success, but it sure had made a contribution.

As he turned his back on me and strode away, I said: "There's one thing about my thinking. It's consistent. You always know where I stand."

He slammed his car door and drove out through my gate.

Clearly, the leadership crisis brewing at headquarters had reached the exploding point. Outside the building, a reflecting pond might mirror its fringe of trees as serenely as ever. Inside, though, a hurricane was ready to lash at the executive suite.

The nub of the problem, at least insofar as it related to me, was that my old-fashioned moral convictions were obstructing "progress," as others defined that word. For nearly two decades I had instituted and insisted on certain policies and practices at Holiday Inns that other businesses couldn't believe I got away with.

Even though I now had a better understanding of salvation and a closer walk with the Lord, "religious" had been applied to me for years. When I promoted corporate use of the word *inn* to replace *motel*, it expressed my concept of the old-time innkeeper's concern for the total refreshment and well-being of his guests.

The weary body needs a good bed in a quiet setting, of course, and the hungry stomach needs a good meal. But what about the drained and frayed spirit? Shouldn't there be a source of renewal for the worried, the angry, the lonely, and the despairing? What better service, for instance, could an innkeeper render his guests than to lay open to them—for their voluntary use—ancient pages of Scripture filled with wisdom and hope?

My kind of thinking on that subject didn't show obvious results on the monthly balance sheet. So, as with the proverbial new broom, some "sweeping" changes began to occur. Sitting at my desk as vice chairman, I heard the new president put Dub Nance on termination notice and order the chaplain program discontinued.

That was also about the time when the "prayer breakfast" on Wednesday morning was rechristened "fellowship breakfast." I have no objection to fellowship as a word or as an actuality. I'm a gregarious person— as any self-respecting innkeeper has to be. I like people, and I enjoy parties. I'm glad that most church buildings include a fellowship hall as well as a sanctuary, and I'm fairly certain that God likes the idea, too.

Why, then, should I feel uneasy about a mere name change? Looking back on it now, I can explain my layman's viewpoint this way. *Prayer* emphasizes the vertical dimension; *fellowship* emphasizes the horizontal. In prayer, you are unmistakably dealing with Someone beyond you, bigger than yourself. In fellowship, you are dealing with someone just like yourself, completely within your reach. Prayer inspires humility, but fellowship inspires familiarity. In prayer, you tap into the Source of wisdom. In fellowship, you exchange opinions.

I have done enough praying to God in my lifetime since early boyhood, and I have socialized enough with peers in school and business settings, to make those distinctions now, but back then I only sensed that something was happening to the substance of the idea. And not surprisingly, it wasn't long before my successor announced that the breakfast get-togethers would be discontinued altogether.

All of those developments about open Bibles, and chaplains, and the breakfasts were only a prelude. The decisive clash of wills at the top echelon brooded like a cloud on the company's horizon, making everyone apprehensive. Squabbles over word changes, the regrettable elimination of specialized guest services, even the major showdowns in board meetings about the very shape of the company as a conglomerate of self-serving enterprises—none of that really prepared me for the magnitude of the storm about to break.

Surely, I never expected a tempest so violent that it would blow me away just short of the peak of that mountain I had been climbing without flinching for forty years. I who had lived and fought for the fundamental Holiday Inns ideal of service to our guests was about to be toppled by a rewriting of the company by-laws that would do a gross disservice to our loyal and trusting public. In my view, the guests of Holiday Inns were about to be exploited by the company they had learned to depend on.

Part of the face-saving explanation Kemmons gave out in press releases for moving me "up" to the vice chairmanship was to add the oversight of our European operations to my continuing supervision of the franchise system. There were all kinds of serious difficulties hampering the profitability of Holiday Inns there, and Kemmons said, "Do for the company in Europe what you have done for the company here in the United States."

I took that as a compliment, and the job seemed worthy of my talents. The European expansion of Holiday Inns had been Kemmons' idea in the first place and I opposed it. But he had made it very clear in written memos to us officers that it was his project and that he intended to run it in his way. I will say he worked hard at it, traveling throughout the continent selecting and buying sites as he always had done. He entertained big ideas about inn design overseas, and vigorously promoted European developments.

But a lot of things conspired to thwart our accustomed progress. We got stuck with sizable losses on operations over there, and we found ourselves holding real estate where it was not feasible to build Inns. If the enterprise in Europe was to be swung into the profit column, tried and true domestic management practices needed to be introduced there and insisted upon to guarantee, again, the integrity of the system. I looked forward to giving it my best shot.

In a sense, it seemed almost like the old days when Kemmons, Wallace, and I were working on a shoestring and a dream that we hoped would pay off. I believed so firmly in the principles by which we had operated successfully that I was convinced they held the secret of efficient and profitable corporate activity anywhere, given the necessary local cooperation. I began planning my itinerary and strategy right away.

The main reason Kemmons gave out for my "promotion," though, was that the company and the industry desperately needed a representative to go to Washington and plead our cause with the government. That was 100 percent true, because as long as we stayed in the "nonessential" class, our fate was sealed. "If we don't get across to them the need for protective legislation," Kemmons complained to me, "the situation we're facing will bankrupt Holiday Inns."

I felt quite assured that Kemmons interpreted my new position to be continuing executive involvement at the highest possible level.

So, as vice chairman of the board, by the end of the year I had started commuting to the nation's capital, there to "pound the marble" as spokesman for the depressed tourism industry—including not only hotels, of course, but airlines and other transportation, and a host of dependent purveyors. I had no idea that I'd be spending up to 40 percent of my time there during the next six years, including travel with a delegation of tourism officials who visited Russia in late 1974 under the sponsorship of the Department of Commerce. During the year 1976, for example, I covered 80,000 miles here at home and gave the keynote speech in fifteen state travel conferences called by governors, usually on the topic, "America's Best Kept Secret," meaning the tourism industry, which was reprinted in *Vital Speeches* magazine for October 1, 1976.

In January 1974 I took a trip to Europe to assess the situation there. On my first day back, February 6, I called a meeting of several top-level executives in my office to report on the status of the system in Europe. Wallace interrupted that meeting to ask that I join with him and Kemmons as soon as possible.

I immediately adjourned my own meeting and went to Kemmons's office. There the two partners told me that in an upcoming special meeting of the board of directors on Friday, Roy Winegardner was to be elected to the board, to the executive committee, and to the new post of first vice chairman, ranking just under Kemmons. In the short time I had been away on the European evaluation trip, a director had resigned, leaving a vacancy that the board was authorized to fill without prior stockholder action.

Thus it was. With that election duly recorded in the minutes of the board, a reception was held in the McCool Room to inform Roy of the action and to welcome him. Between November 3 and February 8, while I had been focusing on Washington and Europe under my new mandate from the chairman, and without any communication to me of the impending management changes, a "coup" of some kind had occurred that placed an outsider in the second most powerful position in the company, and that set in motion actions that would chart a new course for Holiday Inns hardly even resembling the one that had brought the company to world dominance in its industry in less than twenty years.

At the next regularly scheduled meeting, March 16, the first item on the agenda was a report by Roy on plans for reorganization of the company.

Sitting next to Kemmons at the boardroom table, I penciled a note on my tablet and shoved it over to him.

"Am I to be as usual the vice chief executive officer as vice chairman?" He scribbled his answer between the lines directly under my words as if writing "ditto": "vice chief executive officer."

Later in the meeting, the president announced that a new senior vice president for Inn development would be included on the slate of officers to be presented at the May 15 meeting: Michael D. Rose, a Cincinnati associate Roy wanted on board to help with reorganization.

At one point during those winter months, Miss Bailey had recorded in her private journal: "The office atmosphere is very tense and the people of Holiday City are confused and wondering what organizational changes will take place."

Well, now everybody was beginning to find out. For the first time we began to hear Roy's voice in official proceedings, and it was not hard to hear. He was absolutely furious over his stock losses (on paper), as I was about my pitiful few compared to his. He was determined to do several things in order to improve the company's financial situation. He was going to make some more personnel changes. He was going to get rid of some of our unprofitable subsidiaries (like the buses and the steamships, which he called "whiskers"), and he was going to explore new ways of enhancing company revenue.

I could not disagree with him about any of that. Roy lives right across the road from me in suburban Memphis, and I regarded him as more than a business associate who happened to be a neighbor. Roy and I were friends, and we would ride over to one or the other place on our tractors on a Saturday morning and enjoy some really good chats. I had helped him locate his impressive home, and during a couple of private crises in his life it had been my privilege to do my bit to help him. He in turn was most generous in enabling my two sons to get their start in Holiday Inns by offering them partnership in one of his franchises.

For me, though, his whole new plan had one Achilles' heel, a vulnerability that I feared would destroy Holiday Inns as it had come to be known and trusted by the public over two decades of reliable service.

As best as I can research the records, at the board of directors meeting on December 12, 1975, Kemmons, still chairman, introduced the idea of our entering the gambling business wherever it was legal, observing that he knew there was strongly divided opinion on the issue. Airing of a lot of that opinion followed until Lem Clymer, as president, moved what the chair had recommended. The vote was eight to seven against the motion. I breathed a sign of relief, but not a very hopeful one.

Nearly two years later, on September 9, 1977, Mike Rose came into the board meeting with stronger arguments for our amending our bylaws to permit gambling at Holiday Inns. This time Roy made the motion to approve, and it passed with only three opposed, including Wallace and me.

Exactly one year later, on September 8, 1978, Roy introduced another motion to extend our gambling/ casino policy, with an implicit understanding that Atlantic City was to be our target.

The motion passed with one negative vote, mine. At

the same meeting, on Roy's motion, approval was given to carry "offensive" literature on our sales racks provided they were blocked from view with a cover, but the prohibition of X-rated movies remained.

Then a lot of things started to pop all at once. To everybody's surprise, Kemmons Wilson unexplainably changed his mind about staying on indefinitely as chairman and announced he would retire, with Roy then being elected immediately to take his place.

Lem Clymer was destined to follow with early retirement sooner than anyone expected, and Roy would put in his place his brilliant young partner from Cincinnati days, who had come out with him, Mike Rose, the Harvard Law School graduate who had been directing our hotel division very successfully.

My title and position apparently would remain unchanged under Roy's chairmanship, and he wanted me to continue to press the case in Washington, where I was frequently testifying before the Senate subcommittee headed by Daniel Inouye of Hawaii, and where I was beginning to form one of those mysterious Potomac networks that spread out to include even the White House. I make it sound as if my career was in status quo, and that the new chairman of the board and I fit together like hand in glove, but time would prove differently.

He also set in motion the process of divestiture which in a few years freed us from the encumbering Tco alliance (at a selling price about half our purchase price, I understand from hearsay), and a number of other unprofitable connections. Under Roy's aggressive, even fearless, leadership, Wall Street began to get "bullish" on Holiday Inns.

For me, on the other hand, it seems superfluous to say that I was devastated. I can't begin to enumerate the losses I had incurred, the most painful being destruction of the integrity of the system with the denial of the *Attitude*.

I have to admit that I spent many a sleepless night agonizing over the difference it might have made if I had been sitting in that chairman's seat. It had represented the top of the mountain for the past quarter-century, and even for the preliminary decades since boyhood. I hungered for the day when I would be chairman of the board of Holiday Inns, Inc., and I thought I had been earning my way to it by utter devotion to the company all those years, to the neglect of all my other friends and to the near destruction of my family relationships.

As you read this lamentation, you should keep one thing in mind. At that point in time, I still had a lot to find out about the deeper meaning of being a Christian. I was not a student of the Bible as Geneva was, and I had difficulty understanding some of God's truths she was trying to tell me. All of this debris from the company's ruin was burying a man who had always trusted God and tried his best to please him, but it was only a few years since that experience I had at the Billy Graham Crusade in Lexington, and I had no letup with serious business problems ever since.

Consequently, I questioned God with some angry and irreverent outbursts. I certainly cannot testify that I bore all this tribulation with a sweet serenity, a forgiving spirit, and a forward look in faith to what he had next in store for me.

Totally to the contrary, I was furious at being double-crossed, I was bitter about the betrayal of company ideals, and I was skeptical about God's care—all of which, as you know, is a helpful frame of mind for rebuilding out of the ruins! No, of course it isn't. My resentment was only complicating the whole mess even more. It cost me my friendship with Roy, which I miss to this day.

And I know he didn't want that to happen any more than I did. At the time I was appointed president, he wrote to me from his offices in Cincinnati: "The close association that you and I have had in the past qualifies me to feel confident that the right man was selected for this important position. Please feel free to call upon me for any assistance or service that I can render." That was in 1969, remember, and we would part company only ten years later.

When the board debates were coming to their climax over some of these issues, Roy crossed the road to see me at my house and said, "Bill, I've told you this fifty times, and I'm going to tell you once more. All of this has nothing to do with you. You just sit there and keep your mouth shut. Stay out of it, Bill. It has nothing to do with you." He was not threatening me but urging me, as friend to friend. He did not want me to be hurt, by myself or by others.

Roy and I were on different sides of the road out where we lived, but at the office we were on the same side of the fence probably 95 percent of the time. It was that 5 percent handicap on the gambling issue that, for all practical purposes, blew us onto opposite planets.

I knew in my heart, though my mind fought the thought, that the future of Holiday Inns no longer involved Bill Walton. In fact, I had been told outright by my successor as president, "There's no place in this company for thinking like yours." My administrative assistant reportedly remarked that I had become too religious to run a business.

But nobody asked me to leave, and I still had the title of vice chairman—empty and powerless as it was, and I still had the Washington assignment, which was soon going to bring me face to face with the president of the United States.

At last, though, I did go to Roy early in 1979 with my request that we work out an amiable separation agreement between the company and me. It took the better part of that year to develop a document that we could both settle for. I would resign from board and office positions, and would be "on leave of absence" until I reached official retirement age in 1985. During that time I would continue to receive my full salary, which Roy voluntarily raised by $15,000 per year, would have secretarial services and office space for a year, and would pursue the liaison work in Washington and any other "elder statesman" duties for the company that Roy might assign.

Something else happened in 1979, though, that I could hardly believe when it came to my remembrance recently. By that time I was a member of Billy Graham's board, and a meeting was scheduled in Dallas in early September. Geneva and I flew down there, and as always I found it spiritually enriching to spend some time in Billy's presence and to fellowship with Christian leaders of the quality he had surrounded himself with. In a sense, I felt he was my father in the faith, ever since that memorable night in Lexington.

From Dallas we were scheduled to fly directly to Lake Tahoe for a meeting of the Holiday Inns board of directors. Roy Winegardner had written to me about it, concluding, "I look forward to seeing you Thursday evening in Lake Tahoe. Cordially, Roy."

That meeting was not a regular one, but a "courtship" one called so that we could review a pending agreement to acquire the famous resort/casino operation known as Harrah's. I hated that agenda with a passion, but I felt I should be there. Besides, we had to fly directly afterward to San Francisco for the annual conference of the franchisees.

At Harrah's in Lake Tahoe, Geneva and I were housed in a luxurious suite that must have contained 1500 square feet—and I'm a pretty good judge of the size of hotel rooms! Geneva has said ever since that she wants us to retire there, because it has to be the most beautiful spot in the whole United States.

The next morning, I got out of bed, put on my robe and slippers, and walked over to a side window, away from the lake. I looked down on the parking lot and saw bus after bus discharging its load of passengers who had come there to gamble in the casino. I knew the great majority of those people could ill afford to lose their money, and yet precious few would take any winnings home with them. I called Geneva over beside me.

"Pug," I said, "that's what this board meeting is about,

and that's what the future of Holiday Inns is about, and I don't see how I can have any part in it."

From Billy Graham to Harrah's casino within twenty-four hours! I don't want to sound sacrilegious in making this comparison, but it strikes me now that God was giving me a personal object lesson of precisely the temptation faced by his own Son, Jesus Christ. I had just had a spiritual immersion in the business of the heavenly Kingdom, and had felt the presence of the Spirit of God in those Dallas meetings.

Now, it seemed, the devil himself had taken me up into an exceedingly high place, Lake Tahoe, and was showing me that the kingdoms of this world could be mine, materially speaking, if I would just compromise by bowing my assent to the planned acquisition. My position could remain secure at Holiday Inns, my benefits and bonuses would probably be augmented, my stockholdings would surely appreciate with the anticipated gambling revenues (which did materialize for the company as predicted, by the way), and my retirement years could be spent in luxury on the proceeds from pension and dividends.

"Geneva, I cannot do that to those people down there. I am finished at Holiday Inns."

Those words became a prophecy that received almost instant confirmation. Geneva and I flew on from Lake Tahoe to San Francisco for the franchisees' meeting—all my old and best friends in the whole system. I was still a board member of the parent company, I was still the vice chairman of that board, and I was still the champion of the franchisee when it came to preserving the integrity of the system.

That night was the gala opening banquet, the major social part of the conference. Geneva and I dressed in our best and went down to the entrance of the hotel. There we waited with other executives while one hired limousine after the other pulled up and the driver called out the name of the officer who was to ride in it.

The parade of limos ended, and all the executives were on their way to the banquet, while the vice chairman of the board of Holiday Inns, Inc., and his wife stood at the curb alone. Someone in a civilian car pulled up and the driver called out the window, "Can I give you a lift?"

"No, thank you," I replied, "we want to walk for a little bit."

We set out down the street until we came to another hotel where there was a cab stand, and we got into the first one, and we took a cab to the IAHI banquet. When we arrived, no one gave us any special greeting or recognition. In fact, some of our decades-long acquaintances appeared to deliberately snub us.

The word obviously had circulated that Bill Walton was out. I had been characterized, accurately, as stubbornly resisting the Harrah's acquisition, even though it was a foregone conclusion, and therefore I was "untouchable." Any franchisee who wanted to stay in the good graces of the company's present management—and who wouldn't?—must not be seen fraternizing with the Waltons.

After the banquet, Geneva and I took a cab back to our hotel, and the next morning we flew out for Memphis, knowing the conference would proceed very nicely without us. That had been made clear.

On January 1, 1980, the leave of absence began gracefully enough, with my receiving the title vice chairman of the board emeritus at the annual stockholders meeting on May 21—and still entitled to a distinction that could not be passed on to any successor: cofounder. At my official retirement in 1985, it was as the sole survivor of that founding team, thirty years after we had dared a dream that God had used miraculously for only as long as he chose to do so for his purposes—though for my purposes, I definitely would have kept it going a little longer!

Mama, you were right. The plan keeps unfolding, even when everything else seems to be folding up.

15 ★ A Game of Russian Roulette

If old Boss Crump could have seen me now some forty years later, he wouldn't have believed his eyes. That little boy he had said he would send to the U.S. Senate one day was sitting in Moscow in the U.S.S.R.—in the Kremlin no less—speaking for this country and for world peace.

The Lord has mighty strange ways of working out his plan for our lives, and the constructive aftermath of my ignominious fadeout at Holiday Inns was already underway in his timely wisdom the very month I moved from president to vice chairman in 1973, a good twelve years before retirement.

In the Moscow conference room, Minister Sergei Nikitin peered intently at me across the table. As commissar of Soviet tourism, he reportedly ranked third in the Kremlin hierarchy. The fifteen-member American delegation led by the Assistant Secretary of Commerce for Tourism, the Honorable C. Langhorne Washburn, which was sent to Russia in September 1974 in the interests of our industry, had been welcomed by the minister and had received initially what in any other country we might have described as the "royal" treatment.

As our trade talks began in earnest, we were all gathered at a long table in a huge room. Along one side sat the American delegation, including people like J. Willard Marriott, Peter Ueberroth, Hilton international president Curt Strand, William D. Patterson of American Express, and Cordell Hull of Amex International, among others. Facing us were the minister, his various deputies, and the interpreters.

In the opening session, one of our people had inadvertently phrased a question in a way that antagonized the Communist official. For a few tense minutes we wondered if our whole mission was in jeopardy. Abruptly, we had adjourned to eat lunch—by ourselves, so as to reconnoiter our strategy.

My friendly competitor, Bill Marriott, volunteered a tactical suggestion. "Bill Walton has been wanting to tell the Holiday Inn story ever since we got here," he said, half-teasingly. "Why don't we let him do that, and also tell about his peace program?"

The rest of the men agreed. Ordinarily I would have jumped at any chance to do my thing. This time, however, I had visions of myself being shipped off to Siberia on charges of being an agitator or a secret agent! My protests went unheeded. Back in the conference room once more, our delegation chairman immediately introduced me for my speech.

It was apparent to all of us that Minister Nikitin's mood hadn't improved much during the lunch break. Notwithstanding, I plunged ahead on my favorite theme—the unique story of our twenty-year growth to be the largest operation of its kind in the world, opening a new Inn somewhere every two and a half days. I also spoke of the Christian principle on which we based our business philosophy: respect for individual integrity and love for our fellowman.

Then I turned to the subject of world peace in relation to tourism. As I concluded, I passed across to the minister the special flag we had designed for our project.

Mr. Nikitin had a couple of his aides unfurl the flag while I explained its symbolism: the world globe signi-

fying the family of nations, the dove of peace, and the
blue background representing the arching heavens that
cover us all.

The whole presentation must have taken about fifteen minutes—probably my all-time record for brevity,
at least on the subject of Holiday Inns!

That was the moment when the minister peered at me
so sharply. Suddenly, he turned to the man beside him.

"George," he muttered, all of this translated for our
benefit, "when you can equal or surpass the Holiday
Inn record of building a new hotel every two and a half
days, then I will approve your budget!" (Obviously, the
interpreter had made a slight mistranslation when he
said "building" where I said "opening." I just let the
impression stand.)

He banged both hands on the table in typical Russian
fashion, and we all laughed—discreetly. The tension
was broken as Mr. Nikitin displayed a more cordial
attitude.

In the next several days, I would be seeing enough of
Russia (Moscow, Leningrad, Kiev, Tbilisi), both what
the government wanted me to see and what I searched
out for myself, to confirm one overwhelming conviction: that vast land, with its rich cultural heritage as
well as its remarkable modern achievements in technology, well deserved to be visited and appreciated by
other peoples of the world, especially by us from the
West. At the moment in that conference hall, though, I
simply volunteered my opinion.

"This great country of yours," I said to the minister,
"could be one of the most impressive tourist attractions
on the globe if only you could open it up to people. It's
a shame that so much of the wonderful heritage and
achievement you have to share is closed off from our
enjoyment by regulations and limitations."

Bill Marriott yanked frantically on my coat tail. Nikitin exploded. I thought, *Siberia, here I come!*

"Mr. Walton," the minister roared, "have you ever
tried to get a visa to enter your country? You ought to
just try it sometime!"

I hardly needed the interpreter to convey the implication of that. I kept still. The minister relaxed and leaned back in his chair.

"Mr. Walton," he continued shortly, "you look exactly like we all imagined a capitalist would look." He said it good-naturedly, and everybody laughed, perhaps a little self-consciously. Then, immediately, he spoke again. "But, when you talk, Mr. Walton, you sound like a—a—what do you call them in your country?—like a Baptist!"

That broke everybody up, on both sides of the table—especially my Mormon friend Bill Marriott, who had gotten me into this fix in the first place.

I must say, though, that our talks proceeded from that point in a much more amiable tone. I felt that Minister Nikitin had taken a liking to me—not because I had put him on the spot, of course, but because he enjoyed the satisfaction of getting one up on me! Later he would let me know privately that Holiday Inns was the one American hotel company he preferred to explore doing business with in the future.

I had been speaking to him as an executive who officially represented tourism in America, and who knew a good thing when I saw it in the professional sense. I was speaking also, though, as an American citizen who was having his inner eyes opened to some of the less tangible realities about Russia that are hard to sift out from the propaganda and biased reporting that we continually get from both sides.

Now, there is no getting around the fact that the Communist Party, which controls the destiny of the hundreds of millions of Russians, remains committed, nominally at least, to the Marxist vision. Despite a lot of disappointment and disenchantment with the way things have been going in the Soviet Union, especially economically, the powerful men and women who govern from the Kremlin are still to some degree philosopher-politicians. They believe in a certain ideal that they feel is destined to shape a new world society. In the service of that ideal, they are willing to play the waiting game, to make accommodations as necessary, and to gamble on western disintegration from within. We would be fools to be lulled into any false sense of security by their talk of "peace," which means something different in their vocabulary from what it means in ours.

But, they are not a representative government by any stretch of the imagination. They are dictators to, not spokesmen for, the Russian people. Constituting a political party that enlists in its official ranks only the minutest fraction of the whole population, they have devised a system of control over behavior and thought that astonishes anyone reared in a democratic tradition. As a man who has devoted his entire professional life to promoting the free enterprise philosophy, I deplore the restrictive policies that oppress and thwart the spirit of the Russian people.

Yet that is precisely where our problem in the West lies. We don't take that spirit of the Russian people seriously enough—if we pause to consider it at all. We complain about the Soviet propaganda machine that keeps the truth from its own citizens. At the same time we freely make charges every day against "the Russians," as if the Moscow man in the street and the Kremlin big shots were all cut from the same cloth. That just isn't true, as we are slowly finding out through the increasing number of dissidents and defectors.

The Russian officials had a dickens of a time trying to figure me out, I guess. There was that half-joke of Nikitin's: "You look like a capitalist . . . you talk like a Baptist."

Well, I plead guilty to the first charge because my paunch and my wardrobe give me away! On the second count, though, how can a lifelong Presbyterian talk like a Baptist—especially from my part of the country? Well, I think I know what the Russian Minister of Tourism meant. To be a Baptist in the Soviet Union means a whole lot more than just belonging to a certain denomination. It means dogged resistance to the prevailing atheistic and materialistic system. It means living under severe regulations, subject to constant surveillance by the KGB, and vulnerable to arrest and exile on the slightest provocation and without the formality of habeas corpus.

The term *Baptist*, while it does stand for a tremendous number of Russian people devoutly following Jesus Christ as Lord and Savior in obedience to the Scriptures, is almost synonymous in the Kremlin perspective with *radical* or even *rebel*. The Baptists, Pentecostals, and other evangelicals in Russia not only want the privilege of worshiping and witnessing openly in their own communities, but by the very nature of their faith they want everyone else to enjoy such freedom too.

When I talked to the Soviet officials, therefore, about opening up their country to the kind of tourism that would let visitors mingle freely with their people, in order to get to know and understand each other, they must have heard "Baptist heresy" coming through.

That says a number of things to me. First, it tells me that the Kremlin clique sees free exchange between peoples as a threat to their power. Their dogmatic insistence on Marxist theories may not be nearly so much a deep-rooted conviction with them as it is a protective posture to keep them in control.

In the second place, accusing me of talking like a Baptist means that the numerous evangelical Christians in Russia are clearly known to stand for something definite, maybe even dangerous to the ruling system. It is not that they are subversive agents for a new Russian revolution that will take to the street and storm the Kremlin and topple the Central Committee of the Communist Party. Rather, it is that those brave believers teach and preach the dignity and personal rights of every individual under the authority of God alone. Wherever that message has been allowed open expression, it has changed human lives and world history. The Communists are deathly afraid of Baptists and their kind, as they have every reason to be, because of the unquenchable vitality of the human will to be free.

We Christians in the West, with all of our denomina-
tional factions, come frighteningly close sometimes to
jeopardizing such truth that really matters because we
seem to bicker constantly over personal religious style
preferences that have little to do with basic doctrine in
most cases, and that won't really matter in the here-
after. There are some noticeable divisions in the
church in Russia, too, of course. But my point is that
under the heavy hand of Communist antagonism and
persecution, true Russian believers in Christ are forced
to focus primarily on the gospel, putting first things
first.

One more thing strikes me as I think about the charge
that I talked like a Baptist. They do not see *Baptist* and
capitalist as interchangeable terms. In fact, they
seemed to regard them as contradictory. That idea
really sets my mind to spinning, and I am not at all
sure I can fathom its significance.

Does it imply that being a Christian rules out the le-
gitimacy of possessing wealth and influence? There is
absolutely nothing in the Scripture to support such a
dictum. The writers of the Bible, guided by the Holy
Spirit, were concerned less with what we have in the
way of material goods than they were with what we do
with what we have. As I understand it, the Bible
teaches that everything we have is provided by the
Lord God, and that we hold it temporarily, as stewards,
to use it for the good of others and for his everlasting
glory.

Jesus said it was hard for a rich man to enter the
Kingdom of Heaven. That is not because his riches are
evil in themselves, but rather because material pros-
perity can lead a man to assume that he is self-made
and self-sufficient. That, in turn, can make him self-
centered and self-indulgent in his life-style. It is all that
"self" business coming into a man's thinking and behavior, where God should be supreme, that corrupts
and destroys a soul and ultimately deprives it of a place
in the heavenly Kingdom of Christ.

Why, then, should I squirm when my Russian host put his finger on a contradiction between my being a capitalist and a Baptist/Christian? Apart from the fact that a lot of rich men and women are terribly self-conscious about their wealth, I think my uneasiness might stem from inconsistencies between my Christian talk and my capitalist walk. It would have been so much nicer if he had said to me, "Before I met you, Mr. Walton, I never knew a capitalist who cared about other people's needs and rights." What a compliment that would have been to me!

The Russian Baptists long for freedom to express and to share their faith in a saving Christ with their neighbors and the rest of the world. As a tourism official, I was talking to the Russian government representative about "freedom" for sharing their country and culture with all nations. The Minister of Tourism put two and two together and added it up to my sounding like a Baptist.

He was puzzled because his stereotype of a "capitalist" was of a fat, rich man who exploits the poor and lives off their miseries. Talk of "sharing," from a western mogul like me, even in the limited context of our discussion, must have seemed paradoxical to him.

I came away from the Soviet Union and the Russian people with an aching heart. To be sure, our tourism industry trade mission had been accomplished successfully, and there would be some practical business benefits—particularly to the Holiday Inns Corporation, as things turned out. For instance, within a few months I had the privilege of welcoming a reciprocal delegation from the Soviet Union to our Holiday Inn University.

What hurt me, though, in leaving that unusual land, was the realization that mutual suspicion and hostility would keep on propelling us along a collision course for just as long as we refused, or were refused, the blessing of getting to know each other as we really are. From a centuries-old Russian Orthodox cathedral, to their energetic fun-making at a vodka-floated banquet, to the barnstorming capabilities of the newest Soviet version of a corporate jet plane, I encountered a fascinating country and a charming people whom the whole world would be better off for meeting in a relaxed people-to-people relationship.

Is it the impossible dream? Wouldn't it be tremendous if our grandchildren and theirs concentrated on seeing who could outdo the other in hospitality and helpfulness instead of in hostility and hate? Every Nellie and Natasha, every Dimitri and David, deserves a chance to become super friends, instead of being mere pawns of the superpowers.

16 ★ One Path to Peace

Maybe it was that kind of an undefined desire, three years before the Russia trip, that motivated me to introduce to our Holiday Inns management the program I spelled out to Mr. Nikitin.

It seemed to me to carry the seeds of improved international relations. As president of the corporation then, I proposed that we put our whole global network of host resources into the service of what I called "World Understanding through Tourism . . . One Road to Peace."

I never claimed that this would be the only, or even the main, road to peace. But it struck me, out of my own extensive intercontinental travels, that surely it was one promising path to good neighborliness among nations. Isn't it perfectly obvious that the goal is not being reached through our embassies, or at summit conference tables, or in that mausoleum of conflict we ironically call the United Nations? Somehow, people have to get to know people, so they can form their own opinions about each other and begin to develop mutually beneficial relationships.

Tourism does more than anything else I know of to get John and Jane Doe out of their provincial mind-set and into an appreciation of other peoples—*if* the job is done right. But no job will ever get done right if we are unwilling to work hard at it. Cynics won't even try. Where can we start?

I started where anyone must—with what was available in my individual circle of influence. Together with various members of our staff who caught the vision, or at least were willing to play along with the boss on his latest crusade, we designed a pilot program for the International Association of Holiday Inns to consider.

The Preface to the proposal, over my signature as corporation president and that of John Brooke as president of the IAHI, read in part:

Over the centuries, the history of the world has been determined by the patterns of trade and commerce. And now, for the first time in the history of civilized man, the movement of people—rather than the movement of commodities—has become the major focus of international trade. International travel-connected spending is today, by far, the largest single item in world commerce.

In this increasing interchange of people—in their interpersonal business contacts and in people-to-people communications brought about by world tourism and commerce—we believe there exists some realistic hope for world peace through international understanding.

The growth of international travel is paralleled by the expansion of the Holiday Inn system, through which we may find opportunities transcending any business or commercial considerations.

The very nature and scope of our business places us in a unique position for encouraging person-to-person contact—a position unlike that enjoyed by any other company, any institution, or any one government in the world.

Therefore, we of Holiday Inns commit ourselves to a policy dedicated to those acts which will enhance understanding between the peoples of the world. Our goal is expansion of the potential of goodwill among nations and encouragement of individual expressions of friendship and concord.

There are lots of ways to try to make things happen.
You can form a study committee, or a task force, or a
research and development department, or a lobby
group in Washington. Each has its own kind of
usefulness. But, sooner or later, some David has got to
pick up a stone from the brook and sling it at the Goliath who opposes him.

The Goliath of world misunderstanding is terrifying,
and some world leaders, just like old King Saul, have
about given up on calling his bluff. For all my pride in
the Holiday Inns system, it actually was kind of a little
pebble in the brook of world affairs after all; and I, for
all my presidential prestige, was pretty much an inex-
perienced David, marching head-on into danger, and
with a faith that was puny compared to his.

But, as had been true all my life, in little things and
in big ones, I did believe in the power and plan of God
to see me through. If he told me to try something, I
simply had to trust him for the outcome. I could live
with the consequences of my actions as long as I was
sure I had committed the enterprise to the Lord to
work out as he saw fit.

What we proposed for the World Understanding
through Tourism program was a total mobilization of
Holiday Inns facilities, contacts, and influence. This
wasn't meant to be just a pep rally kind of slogan to get
everybody cheering. We went at it with all the hard-
nosed determination that we applied to any other
challenge the corporation faced. There were to be
research and development activities, the formation of
an advisory committee, the creation of special materials
and supplies, and the establishment of training sessions
for our innkeepers through Holiday Inns University.

And all of that was just Phase I!

In Phase II we would evaluate and reshape as necessary everything that came out of Phase I, plus make
translations of materials into French, German, Spanish,
and Italian, develop an international distribution system for program supplies, and cultivate liaisons with

other organizations concerned about international friendship.

There was to be a Phase III, also, that would design a program and materials for Japanese travelers and for Japan, as well as translations for other countries as needed, and that would extend the program to our colleagues in the international travel industry.

I am putting all of this in terms of "to be" since any pilot proposal is subject to modifications as the experience proceeds.

Those phases were steps to creating the right apparatus. The real heart of the program, of course, was what would happen at any given Holiday Inn location anywhere in the world when an international traveler arrived as our guest.

For one thing, we would identify various Inn facilities with international symbols, thereby minimizing the difficulty of language barriers. Our Corporate Identity Department came up with a set of nearly a dozen self-explanatory picture signs to designate such areas as restaurant, pool, rest rooms, and elevator. That was an obvious and simple accommodation to the comfort and convenience of international travelers—and today has become a widely accepted practice throughout the United States and the world.

I knew also that language barriers can do more than almost anything to undercut the pleasure of traveling in unfamiliar regions. So we prepared for posting at the front desk of every Inn an "Interpreter-on-Call" chart. This carried the sentence "I need an interpreter" in thirty-three languages and dialects.

To respond with the help requested, we identified bilingual employees on our own Inn staff, discovering by survey that we had management personnel who spoke thirty-eight languages and dialects—including Icelandic, Hindustani, and Papiamento!

We also arranged contacts with community organizations dedicated to showing friendship to international travelers, and drew upon local college and high school teachers and students of foreign languages for linguistic assistance. Even naturalized citizens from other ethnic backgrounds were likely helpers. For all of these language volunteers, we manufactured appropriate badges.

For the encouragement of international travelers themselves, we provided five-language common phrase books, visitor identification cards and presentation folders, welcome packets, and even a specially designed World Peace flag to be flown outside the Inn as well as mounted in the lobby.

To encourage wider participation in the effort by other leaders in our industry, we prepared copies of our policy statement, a background information folder, and a presentation packet and sample kit.

Our plans included a guidebook, *Understanding the U.S.A.*, and a "Sound of Peace" record album created by our Holiday Inns teenage singing group, The Messengers. Our innkeepers, of course, were supplied with an exhaustive handbook to help them become "Ambassadors of International Goodwill," and the corporation's annual reports were printed in French, German, Japanese, and Spanish, as well as in English.

The first World Peace flag was raised in November 1972 in front of Holiday Inn University in a special presentation by the current graduating class, which represented four continents.

On April 12, 1973, only five months later, I was in Avignon, France, standing beside Mayor Henri Duffaut, as the World Peace flag was raised over the 1,500th participating Holiday Inn. In the course of my remarks to the crowd gathered there, I turned aside to my interpreter and asked, "Am I going too fast for the people to follow what I am saying?"

The mayor, who spoke English, interjected, "Mr. Walton, they understand perfectly what you are saying even if they don't know your language!"

Peace and love are self-communicating attitudes that often speak more forcefully than our words.

Obviously, Holiday Inns was off and running in a significant effort. But a starting burst can sustain something for only a limited time, like a booster on a rocket. As top level management changes occurred at Holiday Inns and different priorities evolved from corporate policies, the Peace program lost internal support.

Today I am more convinced than ever that the increasing flow of citizens from country to country, and from continent to continent, in business and in recreational travel, can be the most natural means for developing world understanding—which is surely prerequisite to any hope for peace.

We should not—and don't need to—leave the peace offensive to governments. Multinational corporations, for instance, have a special chance—and a special mandate, in my opinion—to promote world understanding. They send hundreds of thousands of employees all over the globe constantly to transact business and to interact socially. What plan or strategy do they use to make sure that international cooperation gets as fair a shake as international competition?

My experience in Russia as a visiting businessman, for example, taught me things about Russians and Americans, about Communists and Christians, and about myself. That trip did a whole lot to help me straighten out my simplistic thinking about the "threat" posed to us by the Soviet Union.

The dangers, of course, are nightmarishly real. Our mutual "can you top this" military buildup is not an ultimate deterrent to war, but is preparation for the moment when, either deliberately or accidentally, some error in human judgment or some computer short-circuit will send the death missiles flying in all directions.

Even then, though, we will know in our hearts that God meant it to be otherwise. The legacy of Cain and Abel blights our existence from day to day and from one era in history to another.

But, in between times, we are working on God's side when we exert every effort to develop mutual understanding, mutual friendship, and mutual helpfulness in a world filled with all kinds of other threats to human well-being.

Whether we like the tactics of the antinuclear demonstrators and the peace marchers or not, the question is this: What am I doing, in a specific and concrete way, to create a climate in which the things I cherish most can be freely shared with my fellow human beings? It is worth a try, isn't it?

The Bible tells us, "God so loved the world. . . ." How can we Christians justify picking out only parts of it to love—the nice parts, the friendly parts? Is it solely up to missionaries to love universally for Christ's sake? Isn't it the commission to every member of the church?

As a Christian, I look at war as a tragic destruction of life, but more than that. It is a disruption of the opportunity for me to send the message of Christ's salvation all around the world to those who have never heard. I am for world peace, not because all nations will be just, or because all peoples will do right, but because that has always been God's plan for those whom he created in his image.

If we self-destruct as the human race, it will only be in violation of the spirit of the Prince of Peace, who died alone on the Cross that we might live—together—in our intended fellowship with the heavenly Father.

17 ★ "Wild Bill" on the Potomac

The Moscow trip made me prouder of America than I had ever been. It also made me grateful that God had seen fit to put me for twenty years in a fraternity of leaders like those who represented our tourism industry.

But the main lesson I carried home with me really took awhile to register. There's a lot of dim-witted poppycock going around our own land these days about the separation of church and state. The way some people see it, America's founding fathers were trying to safeguard us citizens from religion and its influence. What nonsense!

The clear and specific wording of the First Amendment to the Constitution, in the spirit of the Declaration of Independence that proclaimed "all men are created equal," is intended to safeguard our practice of religion from state interference and control. I may be only a night school lawyer, but I can read English!

If I, as a citizen, cannot openly express my faith in God, and my commitment to Christian principles, in any setting and before any audience, the "American way" is a farce or a fairy tale.

There is no more logical place to voice my spiritual convictions than in the halls of government, before the nation's lawmakers who are mandated to see that nothing infringes on my freedom of speech and religion. Sitting in my comfortable executive office out in the Tennessee Bible Belt, I could theoretically endorse such ideas. But when the company sent me to Washington in 1973 to press the panic button for the tourism industry in America, it was time for me to put our system to the test.

To represent my industry in a time of crisis was an urgent commission that gave me opportunity to observe firsthand the wondrous and wild way things work there—or don't work! And in the thick of it all, I found a chance to make my Christian convictions heard. More of that later.

It is easy to blame the bureaucrats in the capital for everything that goes wrong in the country. There is a lot of red tape and confusion in the legislative process. But most of those people are sincerely trying to do their job as authorized by federal legislation. They make bad decisions at times, as we all do, and their mistakes can have far-reaching consequences. They are tempted to get cynical, in sheer defense against the frustrations of ambiguous directives and political pressures.

Most of the blame for colossal mismanagement, or waste, or other inefficiencies, can be traced to faults in the laws rather than in the people. Our accusations, then, shift to the politicians. Those wheeler-dealer senators and representatives on Capitol Hill, we say, are guilty of giving in to special interest lobbies, or of serving their own ego drives. They draft laws that are so complicated, with all their amendments and "pork barrel" riders, that they end up with more harness than horse. It is no wonder that federal employees fight to survive by compromises that sometimes border on being crooked.

If we don't like what the legislators are doing, we are told, we always can use the awesome power of the ballot box to "run the rascals out." Every neighborhood polling place is a forum for the voice of the people where they can deliver symbolic messages to any leaders in Washington who have gotten infected with "Potomac Fever."

My own thinking tended to run along those lines for years, until our cars began to run out of gas in that frightful winter of 1973-74. Do you remember the Arab oil embargo, the long lines at the so-called "filling" stations, the stranded motorists along the interstate highways?

The tourism industry remembers.

But the people who most needed to know that tourism *is* an industry in the United States were not the Soviet officials I had visited in Moscow, but our own federal bureaucracy in Washington.

When the embargo imperiled the travel and lodging industry throughout this country, someone in authority there in the marble halls along the Potomac had labeled us "nonessential" and thereby crippled our business.

I don't want to burden you with figures, as the statistician always says before making a report, but consider these few from that era of the 1970s: Tourism in the U.S.A. then provided 4 million jobs with a payroll near $20 billion, and a gross sales volume of $72 billion, making it the second largest retail business in the country.

Nonessential? Maybe it is a good thing I was angry about what was happening to me at Holiday Inns, because that mood sent me to Washington ready to read the riot act to the lawmakers. I pointed out that the energy-saving policies instituted with the embargo accomplished these noble feats in just four months: put 90,000 people out of work, jeopardized the jobs of another 179,000, and cost our industry three-quarters of a billion dollars—with the corresponding loss of tax dollars to the government at all collecting levels. In four months!

A dozen years ago in Washington, people paid attention to little figures like that. But I needed considerable education about citizenship, too. Senator Hubert

Humphrey brought it into focus at the 1974 American Hotel Management Association convention in Puerto Rico when he said to us delegates: "It is the purpose of the Congress of the United States to pass laws. You can provide good information and input and help us make good laws, or you can provide no information at all and we will stumble and bumble along and perhaps make bad laws. But we will make laws . . . and either way you've got to live with the consequences."

The Cabinet and the Congress and the agencies didn't have any "good information and input" about what the tourism industry meant to the economic health of this country. Senator Inouye from Hawaii quickly caught the drift because his own state was so vulnerable to the travel slump, and, even though he called me "Wild Bill" sometimes, he also guided some policymakers and legislators to see the imperative need for giving tourism a new look. I appeared to give testimony before his own senate subcommittee and other legislative committees of both houses of Congress, many times, and I sat in more officials' offices than you can imagine. Senate Resolution 281 was passed just in time to become the magic wand that kept our handsome coach from turning into a pumpkin.

Our industry needed speedy rescue, and the federal government offered our only hope of relief from total calamity. But let me underscore my unrelenting opposition to government interference in the private sector. I hope I made that clear in testimony to a Senate committee on September 20, 1978:

Never has this industry, or any entity in the private sector, asked the federal government to do our job for us. I don't want the federal government selling my rooms, or designing my marketing and expansion policy, or promoting my restaurants. My company is perfectly capable of doing that on its own . . . and intends to continue to do so. . . . I'm not inviting the federal government into my boardroom to help sell Holiday Inn rooms or manage Holiday Inns. There are too many fed-

eral agencies whose presence is already felt in that
boardroom and on our operations, and we don't need
another one.

But those rather brash words came five years later,
when significant new legislation was pending to recognize the vital status of the tourism industry in America.

Gradually we got restrictions lifted that gave us some
breathing space. But more than that, we finally got
through their heads the fact that American tourists
going overseas were spending two dollars for every one
dollar foreign visitors were spending here. That is a
very elementary picture of what the trade deficit is all
about. It was high time that the American government
provided a ranking official to promote travel to this
country.

You might get the impression from all that I have
said on this subject that my motivation in protecting
our industry from disaster was to serve the "almighty
dollar." I heard about a hotel marquee in Miami that
read: "Keep Florida green. Bring money!" Was that it?

There are some people in the tourism industry, no
doubt, as in other businesses, who are guilty of such
short-sighted, self-defeating thinking. I had deeper ob-
jectives, which I will comment on shortly.

When a bill finally did get through Congress, the
president vetoed it. I couldn't believe it! I stormed back
to Washington, made the rounds of my contacts, did my
own investigating, and found out that he had been fed
incorrect information. I gained access to President Ford
and told him the facts. His reply was for me to get the
very same piece of legislation reintroduced into Congress, and as soon as it passed and reached his desk, he
would sign it. I did what he asked, and he did what he
promised. Created by the Senate (S. 347), the bill provided funding to research a possible United States
Travel and Tourism Corporation—like NASA, the Federal Reserve Board, and the Postal Service—as a publicly
chartered private corporation. While that did not
materialize, I was able to serve for six years as chair-

man of the industry's advisory council to the Senate
commerce committee.

Our goal, of course, was to get official status for
tourism within the government. Eventually such
legislation, called the "Tourism Bill," received President
Reagan's signature. I was privileged to stand by his desk
and witness the signing of a bill that established a
travel and tourism administration in the Department of
Commerce. I still hope we'll see the day when the
United States has a Secretary of Tourism to help promote travel here by overseas visitors.

The process I am talking about covered probably the
better part of ten years in all of its aspects, and I got to
be known pretty well around the Senate and the Congress, even though Boss Crump's notion had been a
little different. Even the doorman at the White House
learned to recognize me and greet me by name during
the administrations of four presidents as I conferred
with them and their aides.

In the Senate edition of the *Congressional Record* for
May 24, 1984, while I was still on the Holiday Inns
payroll at full salary as vice chairman emeritus, Senator Inouye inserted an extended statement about
President Reagan's proclamation of the upcoming week
as National Tourism Week. His concluding remarks
included these:

*William B. Walton, or "Wild Bill" as I came to know him,
is truly the pioneer of the industry's Washington effort.
He is a founder and former vice chairman of the board
of Holiday Inns, serves as chairman of the Senate Commerce Committee's Travel and Tourism Government
Affairs Council, and is a member of the Department of
Commerce's Travel and Tourism Advisory Board.*

The very next day I received a letter from Secretary
of Commerce Malcolm Baldrige, asking me to continue
to serve on the latter board for a term running until
May 15, 1987.

That is where the story stands right now. But when I

first arrived in Washington and charged into the office of then Secretary of Commerce Frederick Dent to vent my complaints about the government's neglect of tourism, he gave me a strict schoolmasterly lecture about our default as an industry in keeping him and other key Washington people informed of the facts.

"Mr. Walton," he had told me, "you are the first person from the tourism industry ever to come into this office to tell me about your needs. Where have you been all this time?"

The Kremlin and the Capitol are more than just an ocean and a continent away from each other. And the bureaucrats who work in those respective isolation chambers are bound to give mixed signals to each other a lot of the time because their knowledge is inadequate.

18 ★ Christian and Citizen

We criticize Russia for being a closed society, where the voice of the people cannot be freely expressed. How much better a job are we doing here? Do our senators and representatives, governors and mayors, aldermen and precinct captains, ever hear from us what we know from personal experience to be the truth about things?

But the issue is bigger than that, not just internal to the U.S.A. or the USSR. I'm expressing myself now as someone who has operated a company with establishments in more than fifty nations, and who has visited personally more than twenty of those nations.

I tried, in my congressional testimonies, to project something of the same basic conviction about people that had always motivated my operating policies at Holiday Inns. I said on one occasion, for instance, "Unless we show our visitors a better coordination of all travel-related policies—visa and customs, driving laws, bilingual capabilities for medical and financial needs—we may gain an unwanted reputation as bad hosts."

There is that timeless philosophy again—respect for the dignity of the individual and love for your neighbor. Extending it to our common humanity under God and putting it in its plainest terms, it is "Treat everybody right."

Should that sound so strange in a nation that based its founding on the concept of universal human equality? Yet we in the business community lose sight of that truth all too often, and too easily, by making bottom-line profits our main reason for existing.

If this issue is limited to the realm of humanistic morality and ethics, well-intentioned as that may be, our treatment of each other will show little or no improvement. Added to principle must be power to observe it. We obviously don't have that power in ourselves, as human history miserably documents.

This is where my layman's understanding of the Christian gospel comes into play. At this point, lots of people say, "Just stick to business, and leave religion out of it." They seem to think that our life is made up of various airtight compartments, such as / business / sex / politics / family / religion /. What happens in one area supposedly has no relationship to what happens in another. Each of us is just a kind of walking parts catalog, without any internal connections to put the "person" together.

I happen to believe that God meant us to be whole persons, with all parts of personality integrated and synchronized for maximum usefulness and happiness. The lubrication that keeps the intricate human being functioning smoothly is love.

Surely, though, you don't talk about that to Congress! That can't possibly have any connection with tourism and energy shortages. Well, possibly not, if you think that the business of life is only about balance sheets and the Dow Jones Average. But, as old Ebenezer Scrooge said after he got turned around, "Mankind is my business."

As an American citizen, enjoying not only my freedom to cling to cherished private beliefs but also to express them publicly, I added a dimension to my testimony in that 1978 hearing conducted by Senator Inouye. Fortunately, I had been given an ideal "text" for my message in a telegram I had received the previous week from Robert Lonati, secretary general of the world tourism organization, who said, "The states' position on tourism has too often been guided by economic aspects while the most important impact of tourism on the social and cultural life of nations has been neglected."

I read that into the record before offering my own concluding remark. "Above all," I said, "we must be prepared to love—our colleague, our customer, our adversary, and our fellowman—remembering that God's great commandment throughout the Old and New Testaments, as the resolution to all strife and tension, is simply to love our neighbor as ourselves."

American business, and American government, have been swamped by appalling secularization during the past several decades. To take Scripture and prayer and God out of public education in this country sets us up to take them out of public life as well. When we do that, we betray Washington and Franklin and Jefferson, who knew what they were about when they, without any apology, laid the foundations for this to be a God-fearing nation. While they guaranteed that the system of church-state integration that existed, and still exists, in England would never be copied in the United States, they never even hinted that government here should be secular.

To bring up through our schools generations of young people who are illiterate about the sacred moorings of the American vision, and who are actually forbidden to give any expression of their individual faith in the classroom, undermines the spiritual energy that has driven us to national greatness and world leadership. If we who are called "leaders" in business and in other walks of life, including government, turn from the Judaeo-Christian legacy so vigorously championed by our forefathers, our national future will bear no resemblance to our flawed but faith-filled past. We will be a people in disarray, stampeding into oblivion.

That is why I think atheistic Marxism has failed the

people of Russia and will not prevail to keep alive the spirit of those great people.

It is time to "be about our Father's business," as Jesus said, making the human factor foremost in our everyday affairs, loving God by showing love to neighbor.

So long as each new president of the United States puts his hand on a Bible at the swearing-in ceremony and seals his vow with "So help me God"; so long as a chaplain opens each session of the Senate and House with a prayer; so long as our coins carry the motto "In God we trust"; so long as every citizen pledges allegiance to the flag of our "one nation, under God"—just that long, I am going to consider it appropriate and necessary to stand up and be counted as a citizen who believes in that God and who tries to apply his law of love in his dealings with every fellow human being.

There are some other things that are "as American as apple pie." Chief among them is faith in God. Public opinion polls of our people consistently support that. If we are willing to say so to the researcher who rings our phone or our doorbell, why are we so shy about saying so in the boardroom, or in the schoolroom, or even, it seems, in the family room?

I thank the Lord for men and women at all levels of government who openly profess their need for divine help in decision making. To me, they are not weaklings for doing so. Instead, they are showing the kind of humility and dependency that are reassuring.

After all, that was the spirit among the leaders who brought our nation into existence in the first place. The delegates to the Continental Congress went to their knees in prayer under the direction of a chaplain. It, as sure as anything, is the only leadership spirit that will survive today's tensions and move us ahead productively.

The Bible teaches that what exalts a nation is righteousness. If the definition of what is "right" comes up for grabs, with each of us interpreting it privately, then concepts of crime, justice, welfare, and happiness become actually meaningless and society falls apart.

Government doesn't even make sense if we can't agree on a common standard of judgment.

In America, that measuring stick has historically been God's Word, the Holy Scriptures. The only way we can get back to basics in this land is to get back to the Bible. People who are genuinely and consistently in favor of the bona fide "American way" must everlastingly campaign on that platform. Otherwise, the cause of human wholeness which we represent will topple like a hollow tree in the hailstorm of international skepticism.

It is my firm conviction that people-to-people is ultimately *the* way to dispel suspicion and foster international goodwill. And how do the average people of various countries meet and mingle?

Basically, through travel.

I used to have a very direct stake in that, professionally and financially, so you could discount my enthusiasm in proportion to my vested interests. But that is largely behind me, now, and yet I feel stronger than ever about it. When we can meet our world neighbors face to face, and see in others' eyes the same anxious anticipation of friendship, we will contribute more to stabilizing the international political jitters than any number of summit conferences.

I know there will never be a true and lasting peace on this earth until the Lord returns to set up his Kingdom of Righteousness. I know that there are greedy and grouchy nations just like there are greedy and grouchy individuals, and we are bound to get on each other's nerves periodically.

But if every Christian who travels, within this country or to other parts of the world, for business or pleasure, would give less time to sight-seeing and more time to personal contact-building, I predict we can have a scriptural "salt and light" influence that God may be pleased to use to spare us all from a holocaust. We may not all be God's children in the "born again" sense, but we are all his creatures, made in his image, and it is gospel truth that he loves the whole world enough to not want any to perish. The family of mankind is one, and Jesus died for all. Let us meet each other and get to know each other, and show each other goodwill. That is not salvation, but it is ministry.

I am sorry that, for all the hard and rewarding work I went through in Washington service for Holiday Inns and the tourism industry, it took me so long to wake up to the fact that such activity, too, was another dimension of that plan God has for my life. I was so absorbed in licking my corporate wounds and pitying myself for the dashing of my hopes and ambitions, that I couldn't really see the importance of what God had put in my hands to do.

Don't be like I was. If you have been let down, or tossed out, or stomped on in the place where you work or by the people you associate with, take it to the Lord in prayer and leave it there.

Then get on with being about our Father's business, knowing that "He doeth all things well."

I was never called to be a missionary, but I am commissioned to be a witness. If I am faithful where God puts me, and you are faithful where he puts you, the whole world will feel the impact.

I may be retired from a business corporation, but I am still employed in the King's business! It's exhilarating to be an ambassador for the Lord of lords.

19 ★ Where It Hurts Most

Bill Walton had been riding high in the saddle as president at Holiday Inns, Inc., and was becoming an increasingly influential lobbyist for the tourism industry in Washington's corridors of power. Bill Walton was honored by being introduced from the platform before a stadium throng numbering tens of thousands of his fellow citizens as chairman of the Memphis Billy Graham Crusade and an intimate personal friend of the famed evangelist. Bill Walton dwelt in luxury on a splendid private estate in Shelby County, Tennessee.

That very Bill Walton, at the period in his life when he was coming so close to the top of his mountain he could smell it, was a man torn to pieces inside by an agonizing self-appraisal. He felt he had not fully met his ideal personal standard to be for his own four children the kind of attentive father he had missed having himself, and to be to his own precious wife the companionable husband like his own mother had lost.

Today, Geneva and I cherish each other more than ever in our forty years together, and no couple could more enjoy sharing good times. But there were those few years of uncertainty in my mind about the way I was measuring up on the family front.

Who would believe that? To see him presiding in the boardroom, or smiling from a public platform, or conferring with senators, or entertaining distinguished business and religious guests at Glen Echo—who would believe or even guess there was such an aching heart under that exterior personification of success? Who could know that in his innermost being he blamed himself for making his beautiful wife and four intelligent children victims of the driving force inside him that had produced the outward image admired by many and envied by more than a few? You can call that self-flagellation or breast-beating or an overly sensitive conscience or a distorted point of view—or whatever. My own family tells me I tend to be too hard on myself about this matter. The fact is, though, that I have kept those feelings locked away inside me for years, and despite the impression I give some people of being an extrovert, I remain at heart a very private person.

The only motive I have for exposing such a personally humiliating truth to you, with pain only God knows about, is the chance that maybe the Lord can use it to help even one father or mother reading this to make a major midcourse correction in their family relationships before it is too late.

I have no intention of purging myself with an outpouring of "true confessions" to make your pulse pound or your scalp prickle, as if I were writing for one of those sensationalist tabloids people buy at the supermarket check-out counter. Nor do I intend to get into any finger-waggling sermon about the way you should treat your family.

But I am not writing fiction. What follows is fact. Whether you decide to take it or leave it is your choice, and your risk.

When business executives get their priorities out of order, the place where it does the most damage is at home. Among the most frightened and frustrated fathers to be found anywhere are some of the top corporate managers I know. Enviably successful in their business ventures, they fail totally on the home front. They can skillfully negotiate a multinational merger in the boardroom but can't seem to carry on five minutes of civil conversation with their son or daughter across the supper table.

I'm not saying they don't love their families, that they are calloused on purpose, or hardhearted by nature, or even that they don't try in their stumbling way to live up to whatever father image they know best. For many, in rare reflective moments, their consciences trouble them about mistakes and inadequacies in family relationships. But, in self-defense, they manufacture all kinds of excuses and rationalizations in order to make their motives appear good. One favorite justification is that they are "a good provider"—meaning they give the children a roof over their heads, food on the table, a first-rate education, and whatever extras their income will allow.

I wish, by the way, that I could limit such a description to the kind of people I know best, people like myself in business and the professions. But the impression I sometimes get these days, from my observations as a reasonably intelligent layman, is that the families of church leaders can suffer the same fate. Parental dedication to "the Lord's work" has produced child neglect and subsequent adult delinquency as devastating as anything you will find in general society. Men and women who believe God has called them to serve on some far-off mission field, or in a local church or Christian agency at home, apparently can have a complete blind spot when it comes to recognizing their stewardship before the Lord of his gift to them of children.

This is not a new problem that has come into existence with the rise of the technological age. Two thousand years ago, the Apostle Paul was guided by the Spirit of God to address it specifically in letters he wrote to his younger associates Timothy and Titus. Even in the ranks of first-century church leadership, it was obviously necessary to underscore the need for a man to be the right kind of a husband and father, not only in providing for family needs but in developing right relationships with his wife and children.

After all, is there any divine vocation more demanding and more fulfilling, according to the biblical standard, than to bear and nurture and shape one's offspring into a choice man or woman of God? How are Christian leaders who have founded great churches or conducted phenomenal ministries or headed influential spiritual organizations going to explain to the Lord at judgment time why they forsook their families, or in some cases merely "used" them, in order to save souls?

Parental neglect has become practically epidemic in our culture, especially with the increase of two-income households, with both mother and father employed outside the home. It is not just father anymore who is the potential offender in this situation. An ad ran on TV for awhile not long ago where a baby was left sitting in a high chair at the breakfast table, unnoticed until the two briefcase-toting parents, gulping a last sip of coffee, met as they were galloping out the back door to their separate cars to go to their respective workplaces. They had forgotten whose day of the week it was to care for their own child.

The further complication of single-parent homes multiplies every day. Separation, divorce, and widowhood are destroying traditional home life at a record rate, and making child neglect, to one degree or another, almost an inevitable result. Again, love is not the missing ingredient in most cases; what is lacking is parental presence when it is needed.

Why do men and women who hold influence over hundreds or thousands of employees, or who manage the day-to-day operations of important organizations, or who have developed world-renowned Christian causes, or who simply spend forty hours a week wage-earning, seem to downgrade the priority of parenting the little persons they have been responsible for bringing into this world?

There is hardly anybody who would not give lip service to the ideal, even in this era when marriages and families are breaking up on scandalously flimsy grounds, and all kinds of alternate life-styles are gaining acceptance. Would we view the situation with alarm or regret at all if we didn't still believe, deep down, that the family is sacred? But our noblest convictions on the matter are empty if we can't carry them to fulfillment within our own households.

This is a part of my "success story" that I would just as soon skip over. I would rather gossip about somebody else, whose mediocre record makes mine look magnificent by contrast. After all, why should I bother to discuss my shortcomings when everybody knows none of us can do a perfect job of parenting?

It reminds me of the military trainee who refused to go up for the required practice parachute jump. His explanation makes a lot of sense. "Why should I practice something I have to do perfect the first time?"

Men and women who may demonstrate great gifts and skills in their professional walks of life are still vulnerable to some really rough times as their children are growing up. Even preachers' kids, I'm told, generate their share of parental nail-biting and anxious floor-pacing. In spite of all the pediatricians' guidebooks and TV interviews with child psychologists, all parents are pioneers in child raising, because each personality is a frontier of unexplored possibilities.

In spite of that, don't we cling to the fragile comfort that all the "phases" eventually pass? Don't rebellious teenagers usually turn into responsible young adults? So why should I drag my woes as a concerned father into the record?

If I thought that the tensions normal to every developing family were all that this is about, you can be sure I would spare myself an unpleasant personal exposure. But contrary to certain popular schools of thought that increasingly condone divorce as an easy "out" from marital struggles, I am persuaded from my own experience, if nothing else, that success at home is ultimately more important than success in the market-place. It takes determined goodwill on the part of both partners to make a marriage work, but it's worth the sometimes painful effort if it spares children what I and my sister and brother have carried for a lifetime from our broken home. If you had asked me about that twenty years ago, I might not have been so dogmatic, but I hope I have learned a few things since.

In fact, though, I do intend to show later that there is a direct correlation between home and job in this regard. The priority we give to our family directly affects the attitude we convey to our fellow workers. In my case, as chief operating officer at Holiday Inns, some specific personnel policies were rooted deeply in my ideals about family.

Before I get to that, though, it is worth considerable embarrassment to myself, if that is the price I have to pay, to go a little deeper into this part of my story in the hope that some other family might thereby be spared some needless mistakes and the hurt that comes as a result.

The two sons and two daughters whom God entrusted to Geneva and me are grown men and women now. They will have to tell their own stories, if they want to, in whatever ways they choose. This is their dad's turn, and I count on their having the maturity to be charitable toward me. Geneva, wise and patient as always, understands and puts up with my doing this, just the way she has put up with so many other things about me.

Ever since my own father walked out on my mother and us three children because he could no longer provide for us as he desired to do during the Great Depression of the thirties, I have had a very special feeling about fathering. Those personal convictions have remained strong, even at times when my personal conduct might not have exhibited everything it should.

I am absolutely certain that the presence of an accessible father in the home is indispensable to the emotional health and normal development of a child. Isn't that what the sociologists are documenting with their surveys and statistics? They have produced lots of evidence, particularly in congested urban settings where the "man of the house" is missing, and where "aid to dependent children" is a factor in sheer survival.

Isn't that also what the psychologists are identifying in their analyses of truancy, juvenile delinquency, drug abuse, and recidivism in our prisons? A fatherless situation is crippling in many ways.

But while the density of population in cities aggravates the problem, in many an affluent suburban household and exclusive country estate, too, the father may be just as missing as in a public housing tenement, with much the same disastrous consequences. Even where he is physically present, he often is so remote from family life as to be practically absent. And now, with the increasing numbers of women who are not only employed in full-time jobs but who also are rising to management and executive levels, the family has the added crisis of a missing mother. The phenomenon of latchkey children, who come home from school to empty houses where they have to fix their own meals by popping refrigerated packages into the microwave oven, is a growing concern among law enforcement officials as well as educators and social workers.

What do busy climbers of the success mountain, both men and women, offer to compensate their children for this absenteeism?

Here I can only draw on my own experiences as a genuinely loving and proud father for going on forty years. I know what I have done, and I think I am beginning to understand my motives. They were not necessarily bad motives, but I suspect that they were possibly misguided in many instances.

As a fundamental mistake, although I knew better, I unconsciously slipped into the fallacy that possessions produce happiness. Madison Avenue advertising techniques do everything possible to suck us into the cascade of consumerism. Besides, growing up without "things" in those blighted years of the Great Depression, I had determined, as many parents do, that my own boys and girls were not going to have it as hard as I did. A major spur to ambition for many of us is the will to provide abundantly for our own, and that is not bad as long as we can keep our priorities straight about the difference between a family's real needs and its supposed needs.

By the time my oldest, William, reached sixteen, I had provided the ultimate "thing" for my family—a mansion in a thirty-five-acre forest on our own private lake miles away from the congestion of the city. As a boy, I'd had to live for awhile in houses that humiliated me. My kids would never suffer like that—and this was a piece of property that would prove it. Even *Architectural Digest* magazine devoted several pages of an issue to a cover feature on the splendors of our two houses at Glen Echo—the main house with its imposing southern colonial white-pillared facade, and the lake house in "modern rustic" design.

I shared with the four young Waltons my distant dream of a day when I would give each of them five choice lakeside acres where they could build their own houses and rear their own families. I even paced off the respective sites which I thought best suited their individual personalities and tastes. I could picture myself presiding as patriarch over the generation of numerous grandchildren my sons and daughters would give me. Yes, Glen Echo would be the exclusive and prestigious preserve of my clan.

There were at least two flaws in my reasoning. Why had I determined to build myself a country estate? Why?

I'm sure the first thing I would have told anyone asking me that crucial question was that I wanted to provide a finer house for my wife and a more beautiful environment for my growing children. I wouldn't have been lying, either. But by the time we located prime acreage farther east and began building the impressive main house at Glen Echo, a powerful force known as ambition was driving my own soul and demanding satisfaction. So, it would not be wholly truthful to say my motives for the planned move out to the countryside were purely altruistic.

The second flaw was equally serious. The effect of leaving Pelham Circle, within my own household, was actually quite disruptive. We had to take the children out of the White Station school where they had so many good friends, and they didn't like it a bit. I appealed to the Board of Education for special permission to let them continue there, but was turned down.

So William and Rusty were sent to the private Memphis University Boys School, and Katherine eventually was enrolled at Hutchison, perhaps the finest private girls' school in the South. (Geneen, of course, was still an infant.) While all three have since said they appreciate the excellent education they received, at the time it happened I was exceedingly unpopular with my children.

For me to provide all of that and to keep it running, my viewpoint was that the kids would surely understand that their doting father must spend lots of overtime at the office, and frequently go on long business trips. They wouldn't care about that since I had given them such a "home"—would they? Even if I couldn't be around the place all the time, they would love me for being such a good provider. What more could any family ask?

This philosophy can backfire very easily. I have learned that parental providing can as readily produce dependency as affection. Hand children everything they need and want while they are in their formative years, and they can develop unreasonable expectations that you will always do it. Even worse, sometimes, they can delude themselves into thinking that "things" are their rightful legacy, owed to them by their parents, or their employers, or their government. Like the prodigal son in the story Jesus told, they want the portion of their father's goods that is "coming to them."

We use a very appropriate, and tragic, term for children like that: "spoiled." Too much indulgence corrupts initiative. Where initiative is missing, self-respect deteriorates. That, in turn, breeds all manner of psychological and social disorder. With all of our well-meaning generosity toward our children, we actually end up depriving them of what they need most, which is individual integrity.

When my brother Van was a child, I used to spank his little behind or punish him in other ways whenever I thought he had asked for trouble. Today, I suppose, some bleeding-heart crusaders for civil rights would cry "Child abuse!" But I know one thing. To this day, Van, who is one of the most renowned builders of quality homes in the whole mid-South, loves me and will still take it on the chin from me if I think he deserves a scolding about something. He is his own man, for sure, but he can look back across the decades with certainty that his older brother wanted the best for him.

As I reflect on that, even though there is only a ten-year difference in our ages, I was a better "father" to him in some ways than to my own children. It is too late for spanking them, certainly. And I shrink from contradicting some of the desires they express as adults. Old patterns aren't any easier to break for children than for parents.

I can tell you that a dad's dreams die hard. When my younger son Rusty decided to make an independent career instead of joining me in Walton Enterprises, I had a real struggle with myself.

What more could he want, I thought, than a partnership with his brother and me in a challenging business venture? After all, I had set up a plush office suite for him, complete with a secretary and a WATS line, in one of his Uncle Van's most handsome office buildings. My assets were staked to advance his success. Why couldn't he cooperate with my plan?

There was that old fallacy haunting me again—that if I gave my all, surely my son would give his all in return.

What I have come to realize, at last, is that Rusty has given me something far more precious than servile compliance with my plans for his career. He has given me what every father really wants most of all—the matchless satisfaction of seeing perpetuated to another generation the principles that meant so much in my own development—personal initiative and a follow-through spirit. How can I help but take pride in his successes as husband, father, and bona fide business wizard, when I recognize they are not based on his riding my coattails, but rather on his proving that the "Walton stuff" is still alive and well in my offspring?

Rusty is not my clone. He's my son. I'm grateful for that. But the best fringe benefit for me has been that by my not insisting any longer on his charting his course by my map, he and I have drawn closer together as men, and I have learned valuable lessons from him.

My older daughter, Kackie, is another example. In recent years, as I have been trying to get my act together for retirement ventures, that wonderful young woman was developing into an indispensable administrative assistant to me. She was able to create order out of the chaos of my accumulated files, as well as to handle daily routines of correspondence and public contacts.

Increasingly, I depended on Kackie to be on call for my business needs, even though she lived in her own apartment some distance away from Glen Echo where I had set up my office operations.

But Kackie had praiseworthy ambitions of her own. She astounded me by taking on a course of study in public accounting whose requirements kept her working day and night—as she could fit them in around her assignments from me. She finished the course with flying colors and took her CPA exams with distinction. But her achievement gave me mixed feelings. Of course, I was proud of her fine record, but at the same time I wondered why she would want to strike out on her own to get employment in the accounting field when I needed her help and wanted her on my payroll.

Well, Kackie secured an excellent position with a leading firm in Memphis and is doing very well for herself. Am I to resent that? Am I to begrudge her the satisfaction she derives from making her own way in the world? Of course not. Yet, it wrenched away from me another of those fantasies about keeping my children closely entwined in my own affairs.

20 ★ When the "Boss" Comes Home

The problem, you see, when we have this self-image of being such a good provider for our families, is that we unconsciously develop the notion that they, therefore, owe us something. Rusty and Kackie don't owe me anything based on things I did for them when they were my dependents. By being on their own now, in the ways God has led them, they validate their personhood. Both of them are strongly committed Christians, in belief and service, and are good witnesses to the gospel.

Love and loyalty cannot be bought. The takeover tactics of big business won't work in the family. There the *executive* role must yield to the *parent* role. You cannot draw up contracts or issue decrees that will substitute for personal devotion to the well-being of the children. It is one thing to name them in your will to receive your possessions when you are gone. It is another thing altogether to give them a living legacy of care for them, coupled with trust in them. A man's best gifts to his children are not perishable provisions, but enduring qualities.

Right there is another vulnerable spot in the executive mentality of busy corporate managers that can lead to a tragic miscalculation about their children. They delegate responsibility for that essential care. Delegation of responsibility is standard procedure in the business world, of course. It is axiomatic that an administrator who cannot distribute duties among others is doomed to frustration and failure. Corporate life is so complex in these high-tech days that it seems every little variation in a process has to be turned over to a specialist of some sort.

That is nothing new, to be sure, even when it comes to modern families. Rich folks in places of power always have been able to assign others what they didn't want to do themselves. It is so much simpler, for instance, to put the children under the charge of a tutor or ship them off to a quality boarding school than to have them underfoot all the time. The baby-sitting industry, with its contemporary day-care variations, shows how widespread this attitude has become, infecting our thinking and governing our actions.

There is more to it than that. Traditional things that dads used to do with their kids, for instance, are now programmed as home computer functions, such as coaching, counseling, help with homework, vocational guidance, games, hobbies—it is all coming to be a matter of data retrieval via a keyboard and video screen. It is the computerization of the family room.

But can a floppy disk kiss a bruised knee? Can a computer terminal hug a baby into happiness? Do memory banks record a slow smile, a twinkle in the eye, or the warmth of an encouraging hand on the shoulder?

The machines and the experts have their uses, but parenting is not one of them. Test-tube babies and surrogate mothers work physiologically, but it is not the idea God conveyed to Adam and Eve. I believe that being a father, now as always, requires a man's knowing the intimacy and self-fulfillment of a mysterious physical and psychological union with one beloved woman in particular that miraculously reproduces bone of their bone and flesh of their flesh. Against that background, any man who subsequently defaults on relating personally to his children by delegating their care to professionals is stock-piling personal grief.

In rare thoughtful moments, a man knows such truth. But he usually fails to follow through on it for at least two reasons. In the first place, it is not convenient. Children don't respect schedules. They live in a world of impulses and cravings.

Whenever I watched my little grandson Chase at those occasional mealtimes we were privileged to share during his infancy, I saw how his mother Nancy's dinner got cold on her plate while she responded to his constant requirements. That wasn't selfishness on his part, but just naturally instinctive self-centeredness. As he has been growing, he has become more self-sufficient and less demanding of others.

But a child's demands are exasperating to working people who are schedule oriented. A manager's secretary, for example, keeps appointment books that control interpersonal contacts all day long. It is hard for that kind of a person to come home and confront domestic unpredictability and turbulence. The orderly sequence of the office, whatever crises and tensions it might include, appears almost as a haven compared to the erratic clamor at home.

If father wants to read the mail or watch TV or take a nap before dinner, his youngsters are bound to have their own ideas about how he should be spending that time. Their demands can be more than inconvenient—they can be a downright nuisance, especially if he has brought home from the office a briefcase full of paperwork. It is a whole lot easier to stay late at the office, and eat dinner downtown, arranging to get home just before—or just after—the children go to bed.

Some dads try to get around the problem by making weekly appointments with a son or dates with a daughter. That can be very special, and mean a lot to both. But it is the approach of an executive, not a parent—and it is not good enough, all by itself.

While children need to learn respect for those legitimate circumstances when "Daddy's busy," they must not be so relegated to the tag-end of his time that they get the impression "Daddy's always busy" when it comes to their concerns. Not a day should pass, really, without a father accepting the "inconvenience" of listening to a daughter's narrative of her latest adolescent romance, or of watching a son's demonstration of his new experiment with frogs.

There is a second reason why fathers sometimes don't follow through on relating adequately or appropriately to their children. Sometimes it is just plain uncomfortable. Inconvenience is bad enough, but that affects primarily one's timetable. Discomfort, on the other hand, can really tear up a man's feelings.

Why does a successful executive easily get upset with his children? This question goes a lot deeper than his reasonable anger over their mischief or wrongdoing. Any father gets provoked over such things. And the kids themselves know what to expect whenever they do things that make Daddy angry. But, too often, he seems to get upset over nothing.

I can give you only the man's point of view on this, but I think there are two things that have always made me somewhat uncomfortable with my children—their intelligence and their independence.

Oh, I agree that those are virtues in themselves. I surely would not want stupid or weak children carrying my family name out into the world to embarrass us all. But, it is really disconcerting to find myself dumb where they are so smart! In fact, it makes me plain mad. I don't like to lose arguments with anybody, especially not with my kids. That was true when they were little, and it is true today.

When my younger daughter, Geneen, who is forty years my junior, cites her nutrition studies to justify removing some of my favorite foods from the menu, it's no comfort to know she is right about it!

And it doesn't help matters a bit when she reminds me that I paid out perfectly good tuition money for her to go to college to find out smart things like that. Even in her twenties, she is still my little girl, and I kind of

resent her telling her daddy what he can or can't eat.
(How I crave a banana split once in awhile!)

Geneen, who has always made Glen Echo something
of a menagerie with her soft-hearted love for animals,
is employed in the hotel industry currently and trying
to cope with the human variety of creatures that can
sometimes behave in "beastly" fashion. She loves the
Lord and hurts whenever she sees unfair or unkind attitudes. You can imagine what a totally sympathetic ear
I give her when she comes home from work with her
tales of guest oddities and operations foul-ups! I can
understand her desire to get into veterinary medicine
someday.

Or, when Rusty and I get into a religious discussion,
both of us firmly convinced Christians, it bothers me
that he can bolster his arguments with more Bible
verses than I ever knew existed. He is a profound student of the Scriptures, the lead teacher of teachers in
men's community Bible studies, with a passion for applying the Word of God to his daily practices that often
puts me to shame, and even occasionally confounds me.

With William, let the conversation get around to his
favorite topics of literature or history, where he is as
brilliantly well-versed as a lot of professors would be,
and I have to keep my mouth shut or expose myself as
a comparative numbskull. He can tell you more about
novelist William Faulkner than I can tell you about
Kemmons Wilson! Or he will analyze the Arab-Israeli
conflict, or outline the history of France—in French, if
you prefer! You name it, he can discourse on it. Sure, I
sent him to Vanderbilt University to get a good education, but it is no fun for me to appear ignorant by
comparison.

To complicate that relationship even further, William
is a free-spirited dreamer of dreams that sometimes
appear impossible to an experienced old hand like me.
Yet, that is ironic. I ought to appreciate his vision more,
because when I was in my late thirties, as he is now, I
was in on the founding of a business miracle that every
sensible industry expert wagered would never work.

But I have gotten so used to the comfortable patterns of the business success we hammered out at Holiday Inns that William's entrepreneurial ideas drive me up the wall half the time. Yet, despite all the arguments I raise, he doggedly persists in working to bring into eventual reality his own innovative concepts of what an inn should be in these modern times, even wanting to call them "Walton Inns," the idea I gave up on when I was so disconsolate over my own disappointments.

I guess parents have just as hard a time growing up as their children do!

Such things might not trouble many fathers. But when you are a managerial type, who is looked up to by thousands of workers as the authoritative fount of wisdom on how the company should be run properly and profitably, you develop a self-image of being "answer man" on just about everything. This know-it-all mentality doesn't take kindly to being instructed by today's generation of bright young men and women on subjects like microbiology or macroeconomics that you never heard of when you went to school.

Oh, we know they are not always right, in spite of all that braininess and up-to-date technical expertise. And it is true that a lot of their dogmatism will be shot to pieces, the way mine has been, as human learning continues to advance. Still, even the wisest of fathers resents being labeled by his kids as an old "fuddy-duddy."

Add to their intelligence their independence, and you have got a combination to stir up all kinds of parental distress. An executive gets to the business pinnacle because he knows how to manage and control things. Everything about his daily occupation conditions him to giving orders and expecting them to be carried out. Nothing seems to make people more reliably obedient than the incentive of the regular paycheck carrying his authoritative signature.

At home, though, it is a different game. You can't fire a child for insubordination! You can suspend the allowance, or cancel car privileges. In later years, under extreme provocation, you can even cut a son or daughter out of your will, perhaps. But the executive has to admit his control powers do not automatically carry over from the boardroom to the family room. This makes him uncomfortable.

My instinctive recourse is to avoid unpleasant confrontations. If I couldn't win, I would simply rather not play. If Rusty beats me with the Bible, I'll limit my discussions with him to subjects where I know what I'm talking about. If Geneen rides me about overdosing on calories, I will just sneak into the kitchen for a treat when she is out in the meadow exercising her horse. If Kackie pursues the intricacies of modern accounting practices in the employ of somebody else, I will just let Geneva "keep our books" in her own time-tested and efficient way. If William marches to a different drummer, I will just ignore the whole parade. What I can't control, I tend not to bother with at all.

Does that sound like a safe solution? The irony there is that my children end up with a self-protective senior citizen around who tends to function at home like a corporation official instead of like a vulnerable, still growing, and helpful father.

Sometimes I wonder if my instinct to protect my brood and keep the family together made me overreact to the threats that have come their way. Too much interference can be just as detrimental as too much neglect. The kids have told me in recent years that they grew up never having to fight their own battles. Sometimes I would rush home from the office to bring a crisis under control, or even take a whole day off from work to exert my influence somewhere on behalf of one or the other of the children. I would always charge in to intervene, to come to the rescue, to take over. At the time, they probably were relieved that I did. But now from their mature vantage point, they can look back on it and figure where it might have hampered their development in some ways.

But aren't good fathers supposed to do those sorts of things for their children? Though I loved him and we had some memorable fun together, I hadn't had a good father present in our home after I was twelve years old, so I had to be an extra-good brother to Betty and Van. Maybe I got the roles confused. Maybe brothers are the ones who fly to the defense of their threatened siblings, while fathers are mature enough and discerning enough to stand back a little to let sons and daughters learn how to put up their own defenses—emerging scarred, perhaps, but stronger to meet the next test. Even the birds know enough to push their fuzzy fledglings out of the nest so that they will have to learn to fly on their own.

The business leader, or the church leader for that matter, must not try to manage his children or expect to control their lives the way he runs things at the office. Nor can he standardize them by personnel testing procedures, or define their vocations in terms of job descriptions. In a company, the workers must exhibit certain credentials to qualify them for particular assignments. In a family, though, each child must be dealt with on individual terms.

I've had to learn this the hard way in dealing with my two boys. Both graduated from Vanderbilt University, but they are different in personality, in skills, and in interests. I have noticed it from various clues all their lives, though I have to admit to myself now that I may not have taken it into account sufficiently.

I wonder, for instance, how many fathers, without regard for a son's personal qualities, break the young spirit by insisting he follow in the footsteps of his dad? Papa's pride in the family tradition, I fear, has poisoned the valid personal ambitions of many a young man and woman.

Both my sons had a brief working relationship with the Holiday Inns corporation, which no doubt gave them useful experience, but neither saw fit to commit himself permanently to that company. Nevertheless, I continued to cherish the hope, especially after I discontinued active involvement at Holiday Inns, that William and Rusty would join me in making a new career—for myself, I suppose—under the illustrious name "William B. Walton & Associates."

But why should they? Did they owe it to me? Of course not. Whatever I might have done for them over the years was not done in order to put them under some kind of obligation to me. No, what I might wish is one thing, but what I have any right to expect is something else.

Like Rusty, who pursued his own choice of a career track, William has his own expectations of himself. He has what may be an added handicap in carrying the family name that has been handed down for generations since Revolutionary War times, and maybe longer. I think boys who are "juniors" sometimes are given the impression that they should assume a responsibility that isn't reasonable to expect of them, namely, living up to the reputations of their forebears. The shadow of a successful father can be a dark cloud to some young men and women.

Whatever the case with William, he simply favors the creative aspects of business more than the challenge of administrative routines that always excited me. Much more like his mother than like me, he reads avidly on many subjects, and his inventiveness thrives even through such outlets as gourmet cooking—which is legendary in the family and among his friends.

For William, the most important quest is to define his own niche. It may not conform in any way to my pattern, but, as I said about Rusty, William is not my clone. He is my son. I am grateful for that. I want to serve his best interests by being a true and discreet father to him, not by imposing on him my intentions or my ambitions.

Recognizing that my children are different from me and from each other ought not to frustrate me as much as I have let it. The difference, instead, challenges my ingenuity as a parent. If they were all alike, I could just plot their lives from a copying machine. As it is, though, I have to stretch my imagination and flex my adaptability muscles all the time to respond to their needs. It may not be convenient, or comfortable, or controllable altogether, but it sure does keep me from settling into a rut of complacency about them. When all is said and done, furthermore, I know in my heart that they do love their dad, though their expressions of it vary.

And there is no one to whom I can delegate, even at this late stage, my continuing fatherly responsibility to my now grown-up children.

Especially not my wife. Geneva was the one present all the time I was absent. If she has had to interpret me to them as often as she has had to interpret them to me, she has had a full-time job on her hands—and without adequate thanks from any of us.

But mothers aren't supposed to have to be fathers. That is the extreme tragedy today of so many single-parent homes, especially when you get to the welfare level. That single parent in the great majority of cases is the mother.

Mothering by itself takes nearly everything a woman can stand—or that God uniquely equipped her to do—when it comes to responsibility in the family circle. Is it fair to ask her to be mechanic, referee, chauffeur, tutor, nurse, cook, playmate, and disciplinarian to even one child, to say nothing of four, as in our household?

And then Geneva has had the added burden of being my wife, no simple or painless task in itself, but which included, in our four decades together, traveling companion, hostess, household supervisor, purchasing agent, bookkeeper, hand-holder, counselor, and spiritual counterbalance to my worldliness.

Now that I come to think of all that, I see I missed a good bet by not putting her on the Holiday Inns payroll as my Chief Executive Assistant! This is also the time to declare a self-evident truth. The most accurate explanation for hundreds of public leaders' children turning out as well as they have is that *mother* was where she was needed, doing what was needed when it was needed by the children. I have no hesitation in saying that about the Walton home.

A reporter once fancifully referred to me in his column as "the glue at Glen Echo," meaning it as a compliment to some of my executive impact at Holiday Inns. Now, as far as the family side of the matter is concerned, if he was talking about who gummed things up, he probably picked the right person. But if he was talking about who held things together around this place, the lady's name is Geneva Chase Walton, no doubt about that!

It gets clearer to me all the time. Defaulting fathers cannot lay a justifiable claim to success anywhere. Promotions, raises, bonuses, and awards in the business world are only so much vapor, easily dissipated, if a man is a fiasco in his family.

We hear a lot today about role models for young people—usually meaning exemplars of what it takes to be successful. So we point to certain captains of industry, or barons of commerce, or statesmen in government, or scholars in education, or other paragons of virtue, and we say, "Be like that."

Is there a Christian father somewhere we can point to and say to our sons, "Be like him"? It doesn't sound too impressive by worldly standards, does it? But by the divine standard, it is probably the most urgently needed role model in contemporary culture. In fact, *Father* is the way the Almighty God presents himself to us. Role model? Jesus said it: "Be like him."

That brings me back to the dilemma I posed earlier—that there is no one to whom I can delegate my continuing fatherly responsibility to my now adult children. There is One, though, isn't there? My heavenly Father.

My kids, intelligent and independent grown-ups, are pursuing the paths of their own choosing, and my old authority over them is done and gone. What can I do when something makes me worry about their choices? From where I hold each one of them in my heart, I can lift them up as children still, forever my children, to the heavenly Father, whose children they also are, as I am, by the saving grace of Jesus Christ. In their behalf,

I can ask him to supply their need for wisdom in discerning his will for their lives, for the courage to do it when they know it, and for their dedication to do whatever they do for the glorification of his name and Kingdom. In other words, I can ask my Father in heaven to give my children the very same things that I as his child have to ask him to give me every day of my life. He never fails.

I could have done better on a lot of things with those nearest and dearest to me in this world, and no matter how sorry I am about it, I can't set it all right, and I can't start over. By God's grace, they all are decent people, and I thank him for that. By God's mercy, they still love their father, and I thank the Lord for that. The last thing in the world I'd want would be to hurt my family. I keep on trusting that same grace and mercy of the Lord to help them over the hard spots and keep them on the path of righteousness.

Not for the sake of the Walton family name. For Jesus' sake.

What are you modeling as a father or a mother for your children? Does it point them to the Lord? Remember, you are a parent first—then, only after that, and only as God directs, might you be preacher or president. But those are not family roles; they are callings in Kingdom service.

In the Christian family, there is only one Lord who is to be loved, worshiped, and served with equal faithfulness by father, mother, and children. That simple truth, put into action, will spare parents a lot of grief and set children on the only lifetime climb that counts.

I'm not preaching. I'm just testifying!

CONCLUSION
If I Had It to Do Over Again

I was walking through the aisle of soaring pines I had planted a quarter century ago along the back boundary of Glen Echo. A breeze was whispering in their lofty tops and the scent of fallen needles carpeted my path. I was wondering that day, after the storm at Holiday Inns had felled me, after the first shock passed and the surges of bitterness started shuddering through my spirit, what was left for me in life?

If I had been a stronger person, I would have comforted myself by counting my blessings—a wife and children, a home that was paid for, my health, all those commonplaces that we are too prone to take for granted. But my mind was preoccupied with grim thoughts of the devastating losses I had sustained in what I could poetically call my "plummet from the summit." It is in moments like those that a person awakens—sometimes slowly, sometimes instantly—to discover the real drives that have motivated actions, and to identify the actual values and priorities that have governed decisions.

I had always declaimed to everybody who would listen that my priorities were the Four Great Loves: God, Family, Country, Work—the *Golden Key to Happiness,* I called it. The problem for this businessman was keeping them in that order, with God on top and Work on the bottom, especially when everything was coming up roses in the hotel enterprise.

In any well-run business, we take major inventory at least once a year, and at each Holiday Inn it was a daily requirement because of the constant turnover of guests. Why is it that in our lives we can go for decades without bothering to check up on ourselves? If we would pause more often to evaluate our moral and spiritual resources, and then immediately replenish wherever the supply was depleted, we would be far less likely to get caught short in a crisis. "Come apart and rest awhile," Jesus admonished his disciples. Maybe it is failure to "come apart" for recuperation of energies that makes so many of us "fall apart" when the going gets rough.

When did you last take stock of your reserves? Maybe it will help you to understand what I am getting at if I briefly summarize what I woefully listed for myself in the Loss column.

First, of course, was that I had lost the race to the crowning peak of professional success. Fifty years of expectations, the last twenty-five of them with one company, all swept away in an avalanche of indifference to the *Attitude* that had been my very oxygen source for the long climb. I did not reach the top of that mountain. Someone else's pennant waved in the breeze. Personal prestige evaporated, and with it went the power leverage that people assign, usually mistakenly, to someone in high position.

To keep Holiday Inns on course, I felt, required me to be chairman of the board. No chance now. The company had ignored my protests and charted itself a different course. Yet, even as I walked among the pines, I vainly wondered if there were any way that I could get it back.

One alternative was to start a rival company of my own; "Walton Inns" maybe we could call it. That was the "I'll show them" attitude, but it never occurred to me at the time how opposite it was from the *Attitude*.

To my consternation, every effort I made to launch such a business got absolutely nowhere, even though I was doing everything right, based on those decades of phenomenal corporate growth at Holiday Inns under my operational direction. But my motivation was wrong, and God blocked me.

After all, I was truly his child now, and somehow he had to impress on me that the old lessons he had taught me were the timeless truths that circumstances would never alter: respect for the dignity of every individual (not selective contempt for those who happened to disagree with me), and love for neighbor (not with conditions that they first play by my rules). So Walton Inns never happened, because I wanted to do my thing for my sake.

What motivates what you are doing these days? When did you last ask yourself that question?

Another loss for me was money. Let me give you just one illustration. It had always been Kemmons' philosophy to be "conservative" on payroll (I'm trying to use polite language) but generous with stock options. The latter, in his view, were "only paper." So none of us veteran employees drew large salaries; my successors under the new regime got wages ten times greater than I had been paid. But I did have a backlog of favorable stock options.

As time ran out for me to take advantage of that benefit, I had to borrow money from the bank to pick up the options. That Holiday Inns stock was to "compensate" me for years of relatively low pay, and to be my nest egg for my golden years when my pension would be as correspondingly low as my pay had always been. The current trading value on the stock exchange made me a millionaire many times over.

But the notion that those company shares were "only paper" got blown to bits by what happened when the Arab oil embargo impacted on our business. Wall Street, always unpredictable and incomprehensible, took Holiday Inns stock down from its then current $50 plus to something like $4. And Bill Walton sat in Glen

Echo dreading to open the daily mail for fear of finding another periodic reminder that he owed the bank $1,300,000 in a series of short-term notes.

My personal financial balance sheet is nobody's business but my own (and Uncle Sam's, of course). But I will tell you that in order to pay off my bank commitment, which took me several years and added interest to the debt, I had to sell all my Holiday Inns stock.

That left me with Glen Echo, and Social Security and pension resources inadequate to run it.

"Sell it," was the conventional wisdom and the universal recommendation. Then I could be a millionaire again, and live out my days in a condo at Vero Beach, or Acapulco, or Monaco if I wanted to.

You haven't paid attention to a thing I've written in this book if you think the selling of Glen Echo would be my first recourse. It will be my last, if it ever has to happen at all, and then probably not for financial reasons. My roots are here. I know every tree and shrub on the place. Of course, all the common sense folks are dead right that Geneva and I don't need a big place like this for ourselves. But I have never stopped dreaming, even after my own children vetoed my plans for their homes on the property, that Glen Echo was part of God's stewardship to me for others, not for ourselves. I continue to pray that he will show me how this thirty-five-acre beauty spot can serve his purposes, not mine. And I have faith that the answer to that is on the way.

Turning "home" into cash so that I can take it easy with the shuffleboard settlers on some sandy surfside and have no obligations to my fellowman to challenge my ability to think and capacity to work is not my idea of "the end of a perfect day." But you are entitled to your own opinion about that.

Those power and money losses are the obvious ones, though, that anybody can spot with a passing glance. "Here today, gone tomorrow" is an adage easy to apply, and most people are fairly philosophical about the chances of it happening to them that way. "That's life," is another cop-out comment we use to screen our desperation and despair.

Not reaching the pinnacle of the mountain, though, brought some quite unexpected casualties. I have already mentioned the ostracism by men and women who had always joined me in the *Attitude* crusade, our great bunch of franchisees. But they were intimidated now by the direction new leadership was taking and didn't want to suffer from "guilt by association" with Bill Walton. It is my own conviction, in fact, that at least some of the top officers at Holiday Inns were afraid I might lead a "Franchise Freedom Fight," a rebellion in the ranks, that would leave the company itself in shambles. In my meaner moments, I thought of that possibility myself, but it didn't make sense to destroy what I loved.

Yet it hurt when old "buddies" didn't say hello, or shake hands, or send me notes or birthday greetings any more. When you become a "former" anything, friendship undergoes some subtle redefinition in some folks' minds. Even though I still actively represent industry interests in Washington in an official capacity with the Department of Commerce, and even though I still wear my Holiday Inns gold pin with its twenty-five-year service diamond proudly, most of the old-timers are too busy to bother.

Did you know that Christian friends can do that, too? Forced smiles, formal greetings, unreturned phone calls? My name missing from the invitation lists, or overlooked when important assignments are passed around? With some of them, so much had been shared. But was it Bill Walton or "H. I. Walton" they had wanted to fraternize with, the Walton with a title, with a fortune, with connections, who could be useful to them? They know. I don't.

The bitterness combined with the hurt to fester in me for nearly a decade, poisoning my own spirit, infecting my family, and threatening to kill my faith. Alternately, I brooded and raged over the injustice of it all. As that crucial retirement date drew closer, with its automatic cessation of my salary and employee benefits, worry complicated an already bad situation.

January 1985. My retirement deadline. Ironically, Roy Winegardner had already retired from the chairmanship of Holiday Inns, having worked wonders in accomplishing his goals for the company. He was succeeded in office by Mike Rose. From time to time, I offered each of them my services to the company in my emeritus status, if there were any public relations value in my being the only cofounder still on the payroll, but each overture was ignored or rebuffed.

Then came a phone call from the Personnel Department, asking me to appear on a certain day that month to finalize some retirement papers. A romantic sentimentalist and optimist to the end, I thought maybe they were planning a special little send-off celebration for Bill Walton, the last of the line, and maybe the last of the breed.

Geneva, the realist, kept telling me, "Bill, you're just getting your hopes up for nothing."

Nevertheless, I dressed up in my best Sunday go-to-meetin' clothes, and she in hers, and we drove to Holiday City to keep our appointment with Personnel. I tooled merrily along the road (and still do) in the big black 1979 Cadillac that had been my company car and was one of the primary "perks" of my separation contract.

We waited in an outer office until the personnel person was ready to see us. An explanation was given about the content and intent of the various documents.

"Sign here, please."

I signed.

"Thank you for coming in. Good-bye."

The last active cofounder of Holiday Inns, Inc., former president and vice chairman, with thirty years of service to the company, walked out into the hall, wondering where the testimonial luncheon was going to be held.

Geneva suggested we stop at Wendy's for a hamburger on the way home. So we drove up in our Cadillac, went in and sat down in our Sunday clothes, and celebrated my retirement in a fast food franchise.

At that point, if Geneva had been anything like Job's wife described in the Old Testament, she might well have said: "Curse God, and die."

At that point, I would have done it. Gladly.

My scruples, my convictions, my ideals—call them what you will—could not possibly be worth the price I'd had to pay for giving them priority over company politics. If I had just kept my mouth shut in the board meetings as Roy begged me to do! If I had just played along with the new trends in the company! If only I could do it all over again . . . !

Ah, there was the crux of the matter. What would I have done differently, if I had it to do over again?

That set my thinking on a fresh track. The first thing I had to ask myself was whether I had done anything I was ashamed of during those thirty years and would not want to repeat. I had lost my temper plenty of times, especially with Kemmons, but it wasn't likely that could have been avoided the second time around. I had made some people feel guilty, or at last intimidated, now and then by some of the religious emphases they felt I "imposed" on them, but I couldn't think of any convictions I would give up along those lines. My handling of such situations undoubtedly could have been more discreet, or more considerate of others' feelings, but I would still have promoted the policies. I knew I had not been perfect in judgment or action, and yet I sincerely felt that my voting record right up to the last was not disgraceful.

It all seemed to boil down to a simple answer: If I had it to do over again, I probably would do exactly what I had done, in spite of the costs.

Was that utterly stupid of me to think that way? I have been pondering that for a few years now. And I am beginning to understand.

But before I go on with that, you may be asking, "What about your prayer life all this time? Weren't you seeking the Lord's help? Didn't you remember what your grandmother had always said about God's having a plan for you?"

No, not really. Formally, I might still have been asking God to get me through all of this. But the way things had turned out, how did I know but what maybe Mama had been deceived about God, too. I am not saying that I thought she ever had any doubts about what she told me, but was her God everything she supposed?

That's a wicked thought that preachers and theologians might scold me for expressing. All right, then, I'm only a layman. Why don't experts have better answers for someone who has just been broken to bits by his fall from a mountaintop? Battered businessmen and women don't want to hear platitudes about "prayer changes things," or thinking positively, or looking on the bright side, or even reading verses from the Bible. All of that seems like only a dab of skin salve while they are in anguish from compound fractures of their faith. They need major surgery and intensive care.

Here, however, was my basic problem, as simply as I can state it. I had confused a career with Holiday Inns as God's plan for my life. For me to become the chairman of the board would be the ultimate confirmation that I was right where God wanted me, doing what he wanted me to do.

With that gone, what was left for me to believe about a plan?

As a matter of fact, what was there left for me to believe about a God who had so misled me?

I know that sounds blasphemous, but such is the fruit of bitterness.

But my wavering belief in God never caused him to waver for a moment toward me, his hurt child. He knew better than to put on a little bandage and make me feel good by restoring me to the favor of officials at Holiday Inns, because Holiday Inns, the company that I had helped to shape, no longer existed. It even changed its name to Holiday Corporation, symbolizing the passing of both an era and a company culture.

There could be no going back.

So how did the stand I had taken make any sense? As the Lord brought one and another spiritual counselor into my life, I began to see the light. All through the years, Holiday Inns employees had heard me preach the *Attitude*. What would those people have thought of me, and what stock could they have put in the Christian profession I made in front of them, if I had given my consent to the changed rules of the game?

My stepping aside and taking a leave of absence after I had been outvoted could have made it look like I was a poor loser, nothing else. And I was angry over the turn of events. But God uses things like that in his own way to turn them around so that he gets glory even out of our seeming disasters.

What some Holiday Inns people may have seen when Bill Walton stepped aside, therefore, even though I was not seeing it myself at the time, was a man who believed so much in what he had always told them that he was willing, at whatever cost to himself, to continue to stand for the right as he saw it. "Love for neighbor" might not pay off in prestige and power and wealth, but he was demonstrating that he still clutched *the golden key,* a different set of values that would not allow the kind of exploitation of human weakness that was about to become, and remains to this day, the corporation's most lucrative activity.

To the 150,000 people who knew me at Holiday Inns, and they all did in some way or another, if not person to person, my leaving when and as I did reaffirmed what we all believed in. We had been chartered to care for the needs of tired, hungry, lonesome travelers. Our goal always was to send them on their way refreshed. As a profit-making business, of course, we charged enough for our services to pay the overhead, to invest in improvements, and incidentally to provide a good livelihood and a secure future for our workers. They never unionized while I was in charge of operations because they couldn't get a better deal than the company was already giving them, and they knew it.

Those workers also never had to be embarrassed that we knowingly took advantage of the public, wringing them out and sending them on their way impoverished and despondent—as gambling casinos have been known to do.

I like to think, now that I have recovered my peace to a large extent, thanks to the grace of God, that as they saw me leave, some of those workers pondered and caught on to the fundamental that "integrity of the system" is a personal matter as well as a corporate one. The individual must learn to stand up for the right, and then take the consequences.

Of course, "the right" is not always easy to sort out from all of the compounds that today's society puts together. And even if it were, no two people have an identical viewpoint on it. That is why it is so essential that we have help, and why God has given us both the Word and the Spirit to guide us into all truth, as Jesus told the disciples. He is infallible, and as we grow through our applying of his revealed truth to our life situations, our comprehension of what's right slowly improves.

Perhaps the fact that took me the longest to understand was that if I had sat in the chairman's office at Holiday Inns, all those workers who had trusted me would assume that I was endorsing the new policies. I would be a hypocrite, advocating that the *Attitude* I had promoted was now an impractical theory. I would have so compromised my "witness" that my effectiveness as chairman would have been seriously curtailed if not nullified altogether. Ironically, instead of saving the company by becoming chairman, I would have sold it out.

So my reputation, for whatever it was worth, remained intact.

And the Lord surprised me one day in 1984 with a little "reward" for that.

The man who was heading up Holiday Inns University at the time, Ernie Wilson, Jr., invited me over for lunch and to show me the latest improvements they had made. As our tour took us through the main lobby, a young woman, obviously in the executive bracket, came over and asked Ernie a question, apologizing for her intrusion. He introduced her to us. When she heard my name, I thought for a split second she was going to hug me (which wouldn't have been all that bad!).

"Mr. Walton!" she exclaimed with evident sincerity, "I've always hoped someday I could meet in person the man who is a living legend around here!"

I must say that made me feel good, even though it kind of relegated me to the vintage of Ulysses!

Then a middle-aged man approached who had overheard the conversation. He shook my hand with becoming dignity, and said with pride in his voice, "Mr. Walton, when I was in high school, I was a member of your singing group, The Messengers."

Small things, to be sure, but tokens that certain seeds planted in the past had taken root and kept growing. That's a real comfort to me.

There still remained, though, that conundrum about the plan. If Holiday Inns was not it, what was? Why had God let me spend myself there for thirty years if he had something different in mind?

Today, slow learner that I am, another truth is dawning. Again, I hope I can make it clear to you by a simple play on words. *Location* is not the same as *Vocation.*

God's plan for each and every one of us is a sacred vocation, the "high calling" of which Scripture speaks. We are agents of his heavenly Kingdom here on earth, representatives of righteousness, for as long as he sees fit to leave us here. Every Christian's vocation is the same: "You shall be witnesses to me" is the way Jesus put it. That is the *Why* of our work on earth.

The *Where* of our witnessing is the location, and that is different for each one of us, although it is all under God's sovereign appointment. That is why I referred to the "myth" of a so-called Christian company. A business corporation is only a legal entity without a personality and without a life of its own.

God has chosen to place some of us there as our location, the site of our service, just as some have been placed in schools or in politics or in church organizations or in sanitation crews or in sales or on a foreign mission field. We Christians are all in the same vocation, but we practice it in a variety of locations.

So Holiday Inns was neither the *Why* nor the *What* of God's plan for me; it was the *Where*. Once I understood that, I began to feel the revival of hope. Why? Because I knew God's plan for Bill Walton did not end the day I resigned from the board and vice chairmanship, or the day I drove from Holiday City to Wendy's. My life still had a holy purpose in the mind of the Lord, and he would still be using the talents and experience he had given me to work it out. The *Why* and the *What* are intact to this very moment. A businessman is what I am, and he is not likely to turn me into a ballet dancer! (I feel very confident about that.)

The question facing me now is, Where, Lord? What's the next location for my vocation? Is it the pages of this book? Is it making speeches at Christian conventions (as I've done several times in the past few years)? Wherever you place me, Lord, it will be to witness for Jesus Christ with the story of your faithfulness that you have given me to tell.

That should make a good closing sentence for this book—a high note of spiritual inspiration that makes it sound as if I have made it to maturity at last. A bold declaration of clear understanding and firm dedication.

But even since I reached this point, God has updated his dealings with this wayfarer named Walton in moves that stagger my imagination. I'm not sure but what his divine sense of humor plays as big a part in recent developments as his divine purpose and power! Let me fill you in.

In 1985, after my official retirement from the company, and after I reached a better attitude in trusting the Lord with my future, admitting to him that I had finally faced and accepted the harsh reality of unful-

filled dreams, and had given up my personal ambitions,
this is what he did.

First, he turned the tables on me—on me who had
organized the largest franchise system in the history of
the lodging industry—and made me a franchise holder
myself. The opportunity came through my friend Bob
Brock in Dallas, who had retained me as consultant to
his hotel chain to purchase a choice franchise from
him and build a Residence Inn in North Charleston,
South Carolina.

It's almost as if it fell into my lap like a ripe apple
after I had given up years of scrambling and skinning
my shins to get a hotel of my own started.

You never can tell what the Lord will give you when
you leave the choice to him. But I was still responsible
to work out the details of locating the best possible site,
working through all the zoning regulations, talking to
contractors and getting bids, arranging for management
of the inn by the kind of people I could count on, and
agonizing to secure the financing (which eventually
was provided by one of America's major banks on a
signature loan that ran close to seven figures). All of
that took months and months, trying my patience and
straining my own resources. Yes, testing my faith, if
you please.

In November 1986 we dedicated the new inn with
occupancy of the suites at 100 percent. Isaiah, an
experienced maintenance engineer and an ordained
minister, left a job elsewhere and joined our staff because, as he explained to me, he wanted to work at a
place where no liquor was sold. Ruth, a mature Christian woman recovering from the bereavement of her
husband, read advance stories about the opening in the
newspapers and turned up to become hostess in our
reception area called the Gatehouse. A superbly qualified man named Mark Snyder, completely sympathetic
to my ideals, took on the responsibility of resident
manager.

This inn not only reinstates me in the hotel business,
with the ironic twist that I am now a franchisee instead

of a company executive, but it promises to solve a serious financial dilemma that had nagged me ever since I had paid my way past the "easy out" of declaring bankruptcy.

And the Lord wasn't through surprising me yet! Bob Brock developed a new lodging system called Park Inns International, and almost before I could get used to the idea of holding a franchise, my old friend decided my consultant role was finished. As 1987 dawned, he brought me into association with Park Inns to wear the title Chairman of the Board. The top of the mountain— as God chose!

At the very same time in Holiday Corporation, takeover threats had prompted top executives to consider drastic restructuring options to defend themselves. In the front page lead story in the *Wall Street Journal* on February 11, 1987, reporter John Helyar reviewed the company's history from its beginning in the 1950s through its current corporate dilemma, and drew this conclusion: "The preoccupation with financial maneuverings is a far cry from the early entrepreneurial days and a source of concern for many, who fear that the good times have forever gone the way of 'the Great Sign.' "

And I, by the grace and goodness of God, am being given a fresh chance to contribute in building a major service organization that will reaffirm those old biblical truths about love for God and love for neighbor as the key to a genuine "success." Above everything else, it gives proof that his love for us is the master key to survival of the human spirit, through whatever circumstances life may bring our way. The Lord can use that to baffle a world system that distorts the value of a soul by rating dollar profits higher than human sanctity in the loving purpose of God.

I can't tell any other man or woman's story but my own. That is what you have just had the patience to read. As the good Lord sees fit to spare my life, the story will have a sequel, whether written or not, because he is going to keep on working in me, and I am going to keep on duty for him. It doesn't matter that I have passed into retirement age chronologically, because my true life is eternal and my service for Christ and his Kingdom will be unending—in the hotel business or out of it, as he determines.

We Christians, therefore, are the most fortunate people on the face of the earth. Not just because we have been granted salvation through the sacrifice of Jesus for us on the cross. Not just because we are part of a great fellowship of believers in Christ that encircles the globe and embraces peoples of all nations and tongues.

But we are each personally most fortunate in that our individual lives keep on counting! Keep on mattering! Keep on making a difference in this godless world because, as Jesus told us, we are salt and light!

You may be a teenager or a senior citizen, an athlete or an invalid, a truck driver or a tapestry weaver, a mother or a father, a business tycoon or a starving artist—keep the catalog of occupations going as far as you want to extend it—the point is that in the plan of God *you* are vital to his work.

So now, as I am approaching my three score years and ten on this earth, I'm getting smarter! Isn't that a consolation! And after fussing for a decade about the raw deal I got from the people who I thought owed me so much, I am waking up to the fact that Holiday Inns, Inc., much as I enjoyed the work and loved the people, was not my life, nor even God's plan for my life, but was only my temporary placement. There, God allowed me to work with him, I believe, to let a few travelers know that there is a caring Companion along life's highway who wants to help us all get Home safely. Now, for awhile at least, he is letting me do again what I know best how to do.

Are all my questions answered? Not by a country mile. I have plenty of questions left. But they no longer are dredged up from anxiety and doubt. They spring from anticipation and delight.

With *the golden key* of God's love in my hand, I need not be daunted by any locked doors I may face.

The Lord transferred me before I got to the top of the one particular mountain I had chosen to climb, the Success Mountain, where I had mistaken Holiday Inns board chairmanship as my destination. I can see now that I did not suffer a fatal fall.

Today, he and I are going on together in the lifelong climb to a heavenly gate that the key of divine love will open on everlasting splendors such as the human mind cannot conceive, and on everlasting service that will be an infinite extension of what he knows I can do and has been training me for all the while I'm here.

It's a great life.

It's a great plan.

Where to, Lord? What next?